LANDSCAPES IN OILS

FRED HEWISON

Copyright © Fred Hewison 2023

All rights reserved.
No part of this publication
may be reproduced, distributed,
or transmitted in any form or by
any means, including photocopying,
recording, or other electronic
or mechanical methods, without
the prior written permission of
the publisher, except in the case
of brief quotations embodied in
critical reviews and certain other
non-commercial uses permitted
by copyright law.

 A catalogue record for this work is available from the National Library of Australia

Hewison, Fred (author)
LANDSCAPES IN OILS
ISBN 978-1-922957-05-4

Cover and book design by

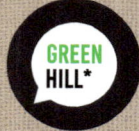

This book is dedicated to my beautiful wife Margaret
whose critique I value more than any
and the master artist Robert Wilson,
whose tutelage, honesty and artistic wisdom
has made my journey so enjoyable.

F.H.

PREFACE

Although I have enjoyed painting in oils since mid-1970 and of a variety of subjects, this book includes mostly those that I have painted whilst living in Banora Point, in Tweed Heads, near the Queensland border. Many of my earlier paintings were of the New South Wales Central Coast when living at Copacabana near Gosford, during which I was an enthusiastic and prominent member of the Central Coast Art Society. I regret that I kept very few records of the many paintings I completed of those beautiful coastal scenes that that area provided but with most things, it is just as well not to dwell on the past.

There is a preponderance of paintings included in this book of the surrounding area in which my wife and I now live. This should not be surprising, as any landscape artist living in such an area as this, would find it hardly necessary to travel too far to find a wealth of subjects that present themselves. So is the reason for the frequent inclusion of the soaring Mount Warning, the beautiful Tweed River and the Border Ranges, which I hope have been depicted in all their glory with the keynote of 'simplicity' and not 'complexity.'

Such is the might of Mount Warning, that the wonderful landscape artist, Elioth Gruner was commissioned in 1919 by the Art Gallery of New South Wales, to paint his *The Valley of the Tweed*, which he completed in 1921.

One can only wonder at the exhaustive effort it surely must have taken to scale the escarpment and produce such a grand masterpiece that depicts Mount Warning — the core of the largest extinct volcano in the southern hemisphere, with its lush rolling pastures and gigantic caldera.

There are also many inclusions of the Clarence River at Grafton and its outskirts. These were the result of my regular attendance at the annual *Grafton Artsfest*, whereat many of Australia's finest artists, including Robert Wilson, were invited or selected to tutor the many aspiring and eager attendees.

I find it necessary to admit that I have not visited the sites of two paintings I have included viz. '*Mount Egmont, NZ*' and '*King George Falls*', but were painted on consignment.
I thought they were still worthy of inclusion, anyway.

As I imagine most artists do - I paint for the simple pleasure it brings to my life, for whilst we artists all encounter those frustrations and disappointments along the way, it is often overcome by a deft brushstroke or two that will produce a personally perceived 'masterpiece' — and what more would any artist strive for, or even expect?

In finality, I must thank the wonderful Australian master-artist and good friend, Robert Wilson, whose tutelage, honesty and professional wisdom has been so invaluable during my journey. It is something I shall not forget.

But last and certainly not least, I am in debt to my dear wife, Margaret, who may have at times been somewhat overgenerous in her summation of my paintings. But as with any artist, a little praise goes a long way and without her continuing support, I can only wonder whether this book might have seen the light of day.

Fred Hewison

Tweed River, Tumbulgum, NSW

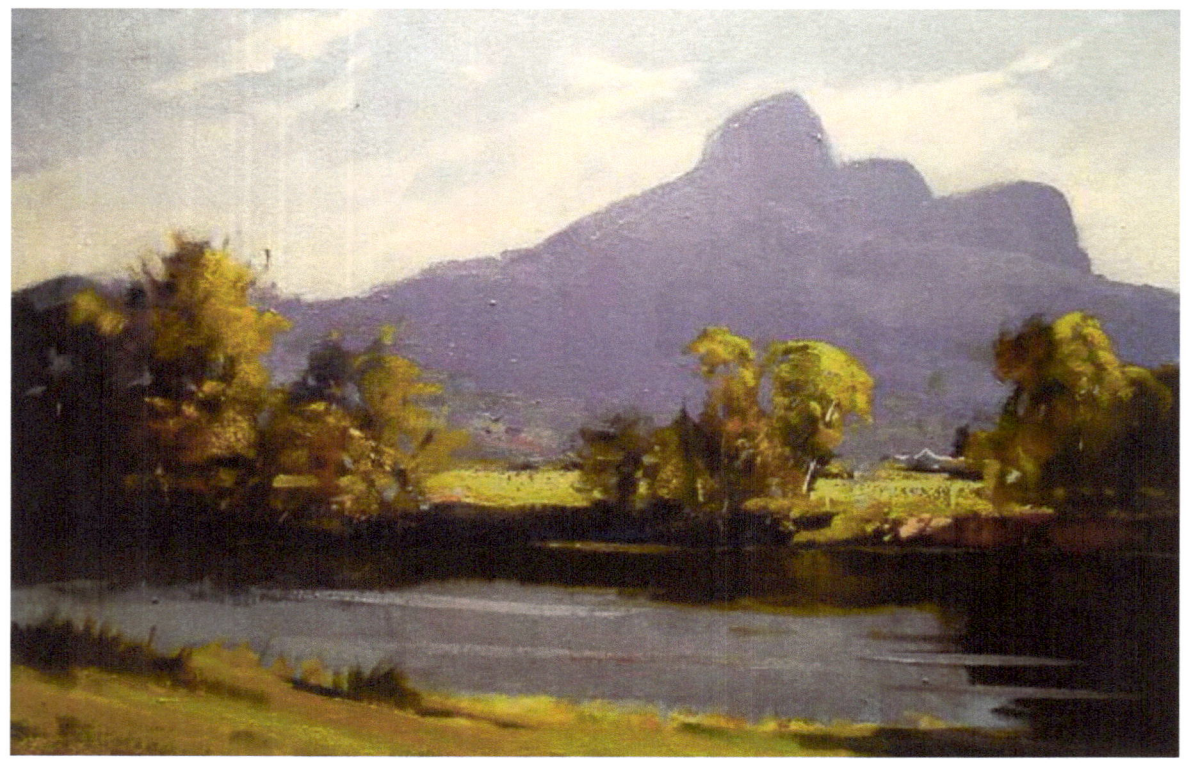

Namoi River, Manilla, NSW

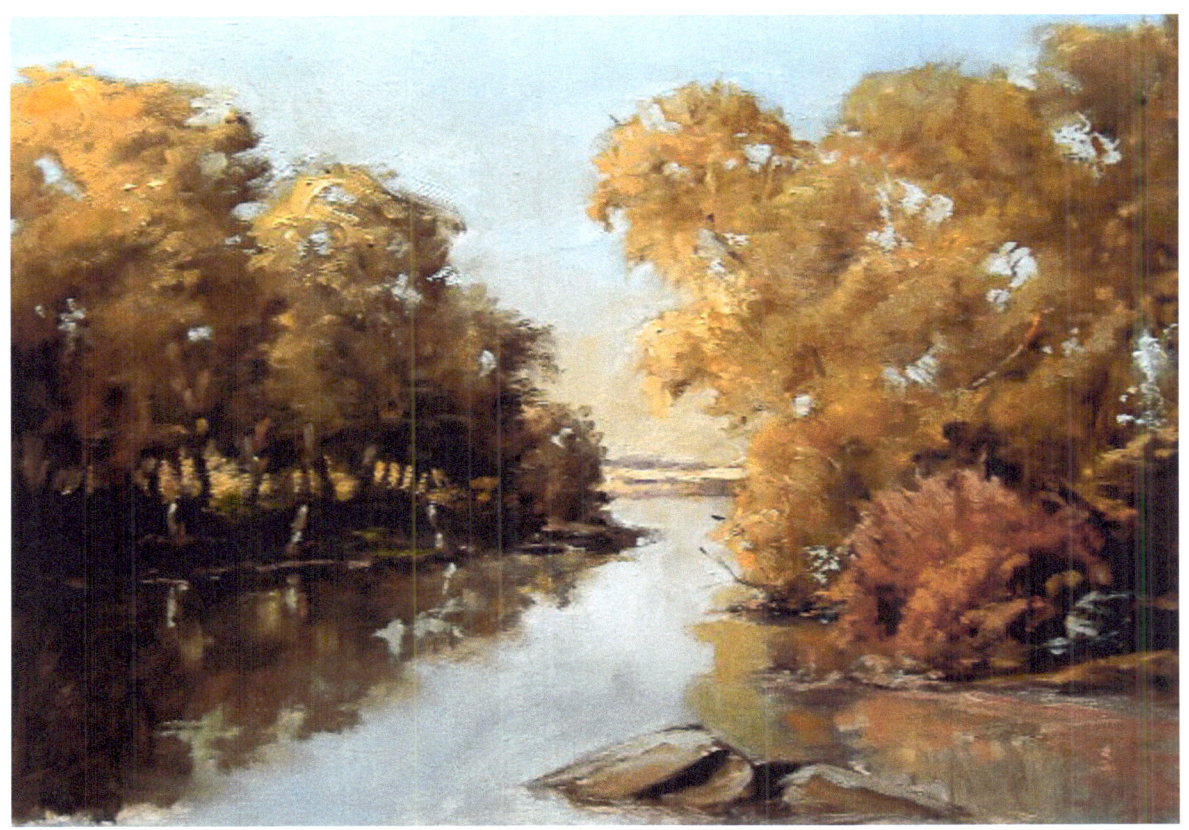

Old Canefield, Murwillumbah, NSW

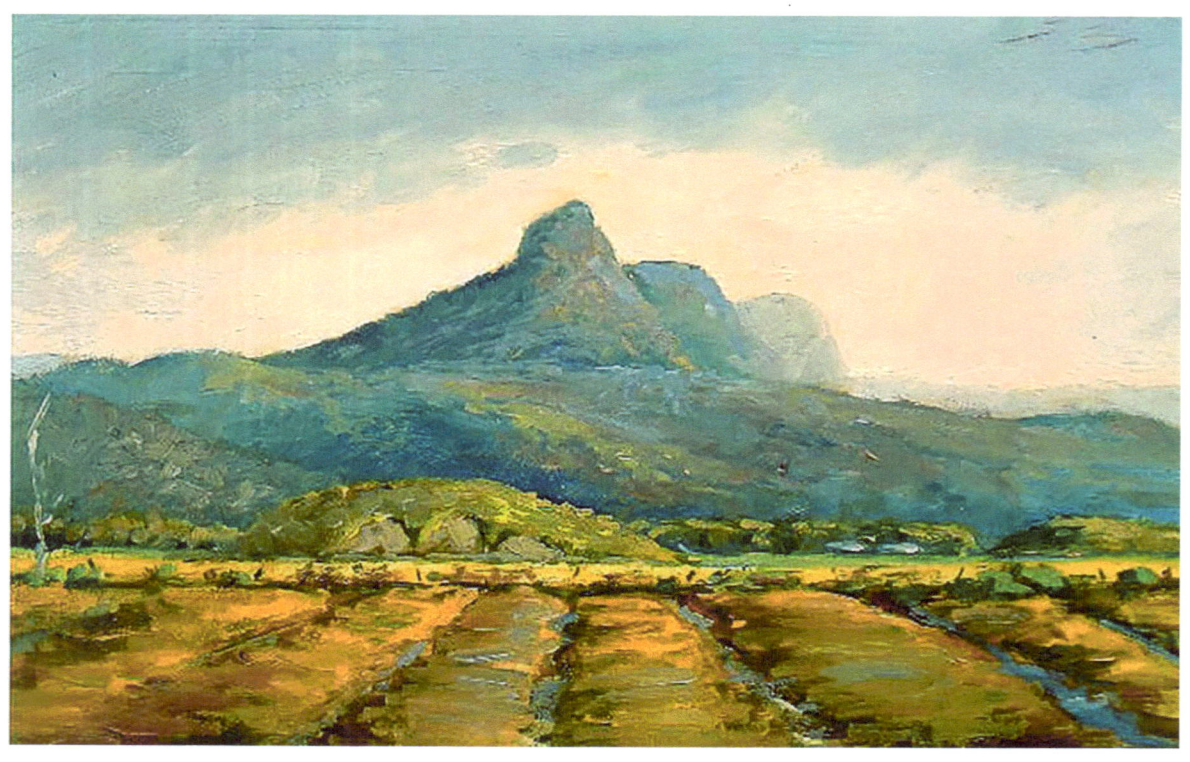

South from Terrar ora

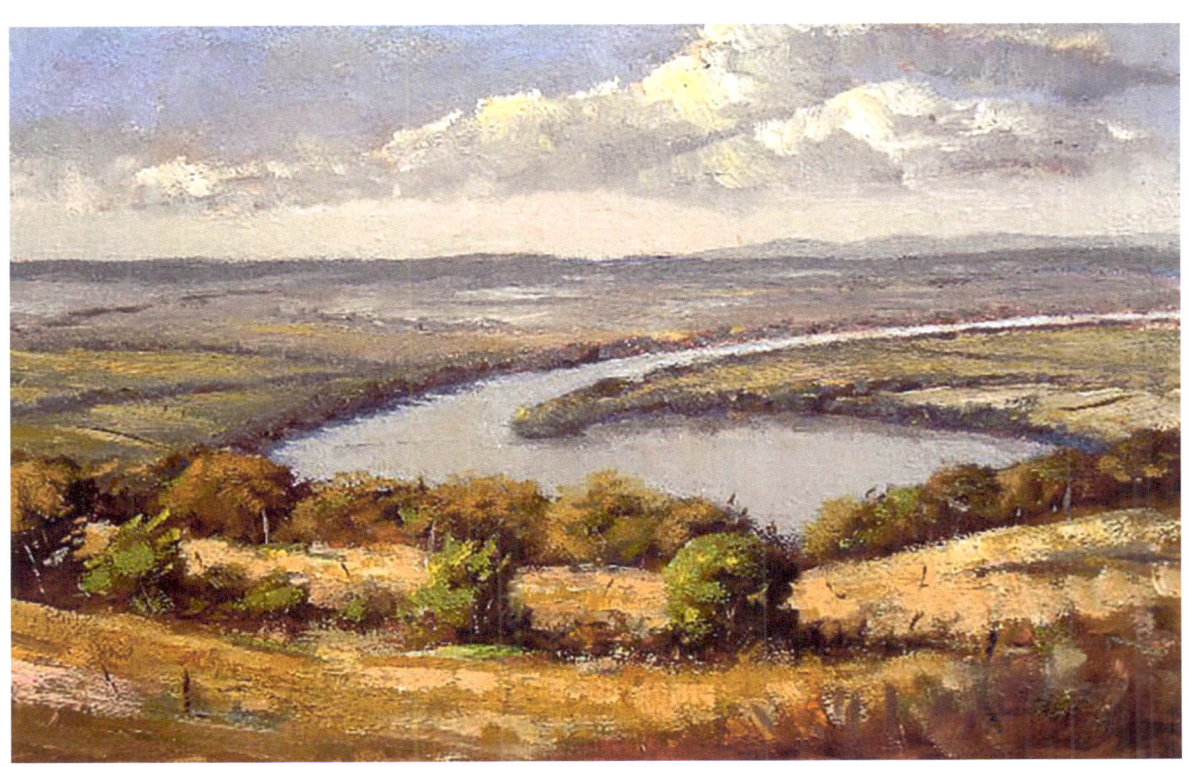

Copmanhurst, Grafton

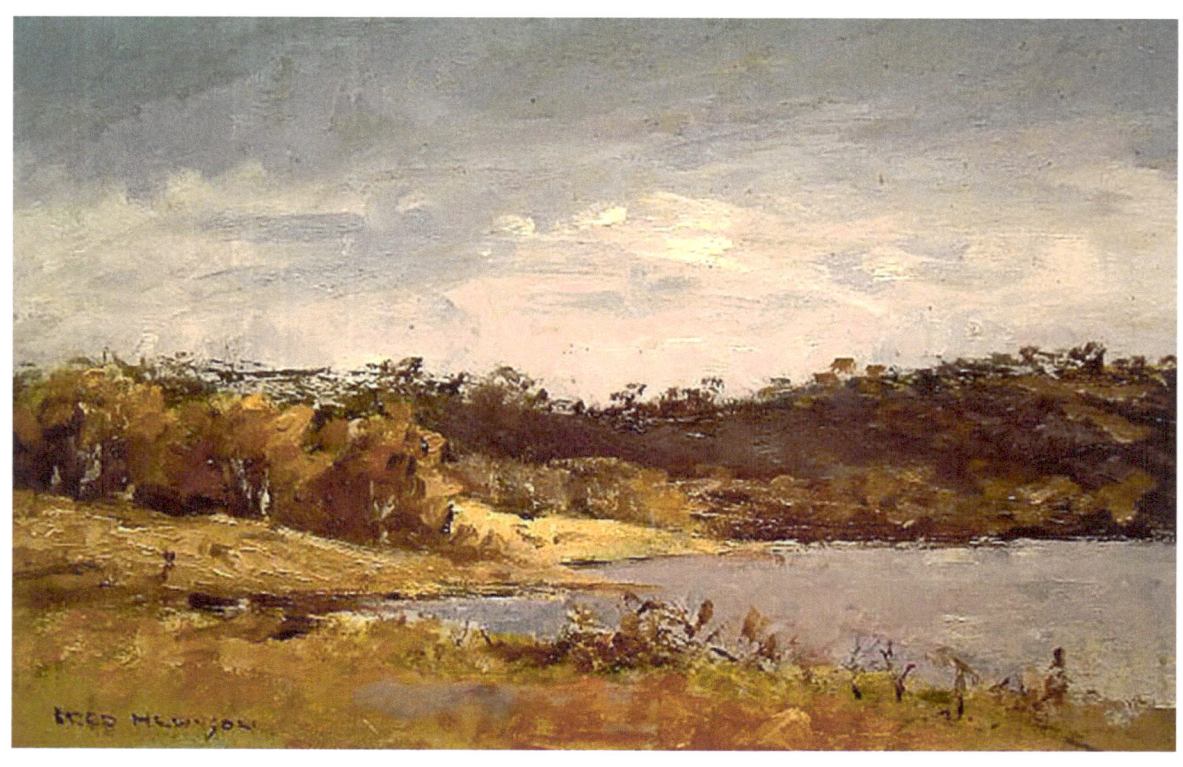

Tweed River, Murwillumbah, NSW

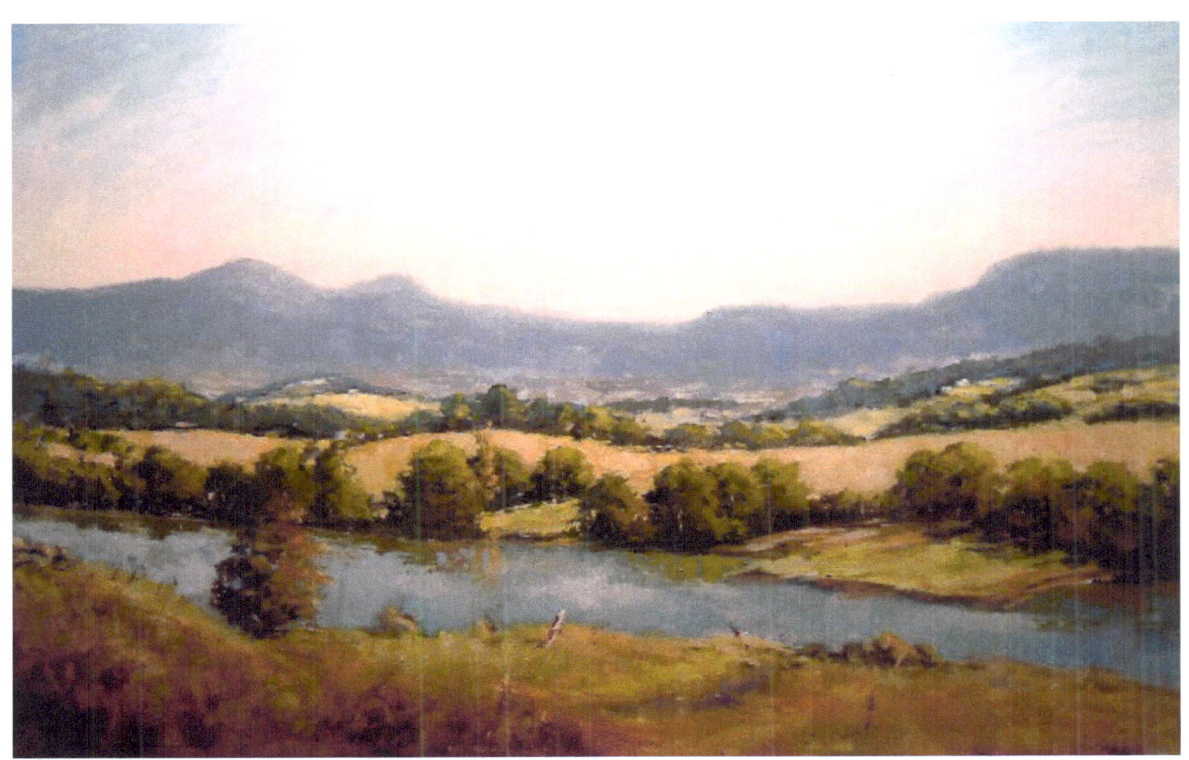

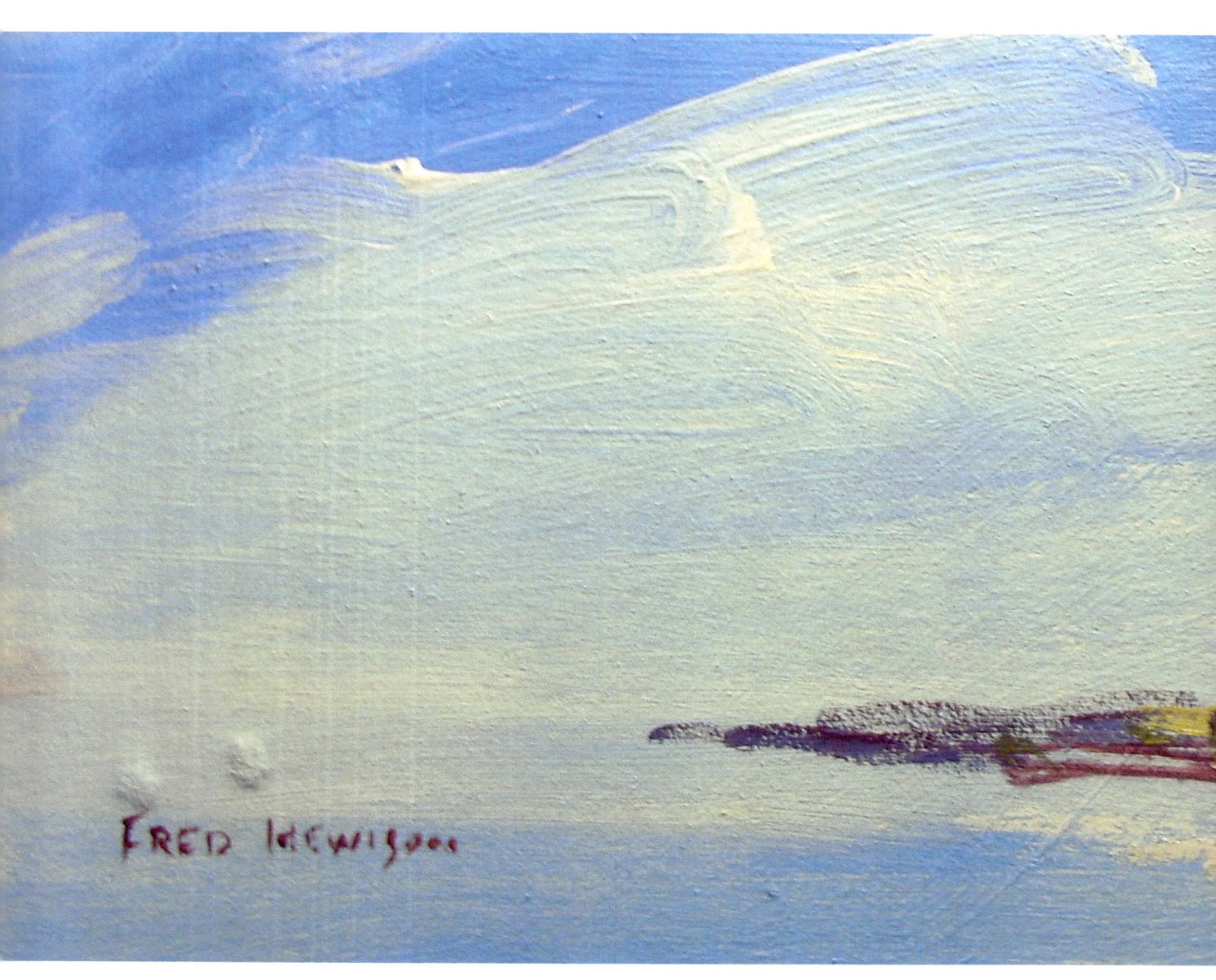

An idea

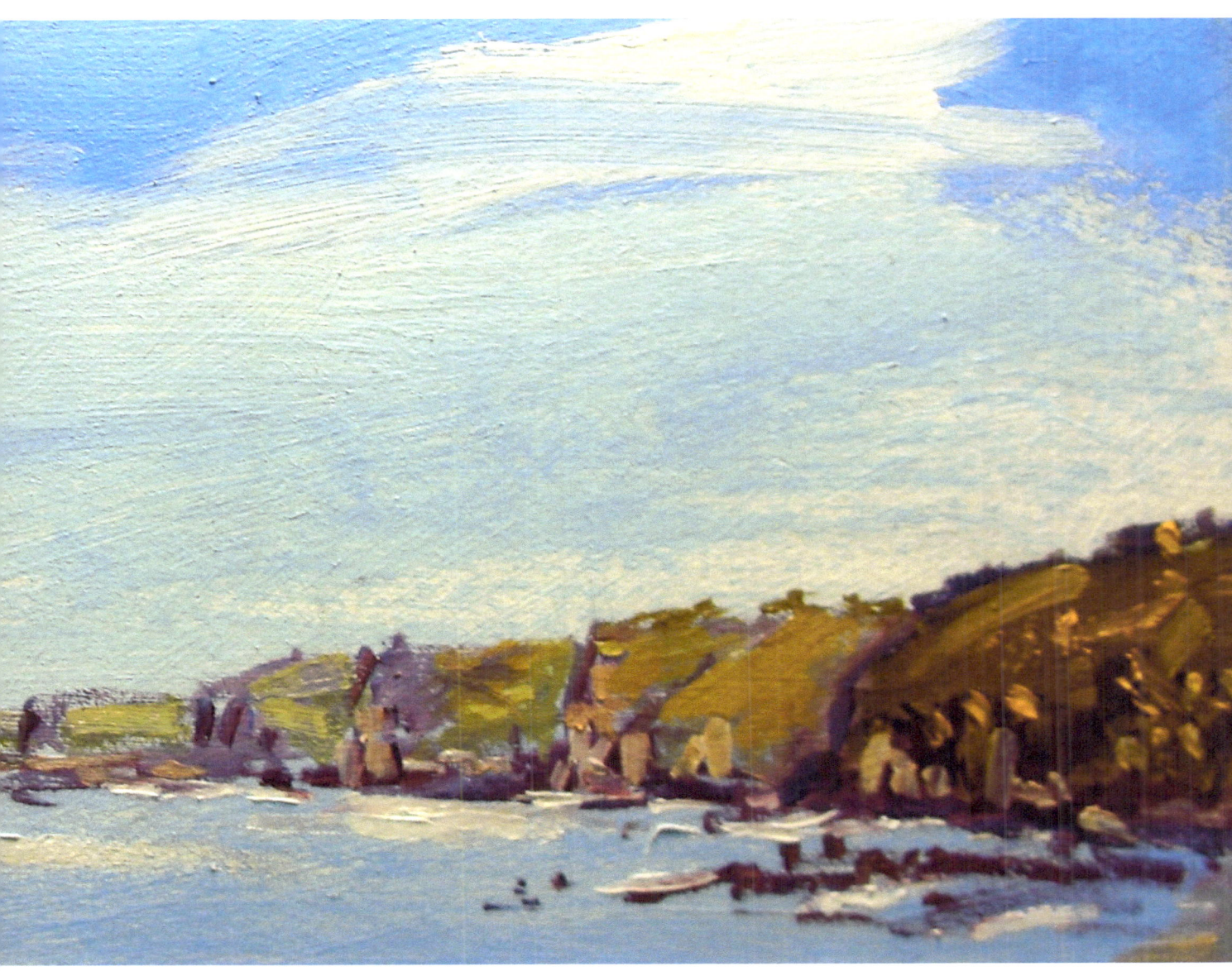

Clarence River, Grafton

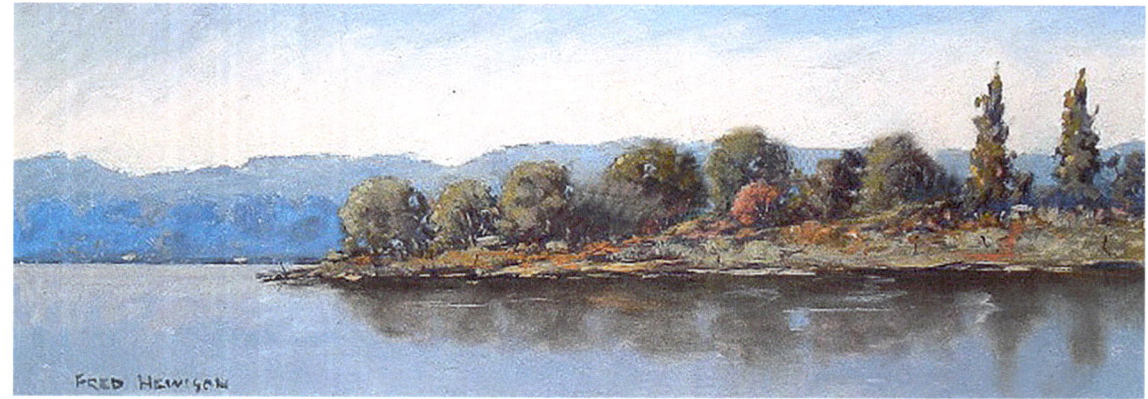

Kangaroo Creek, NSW

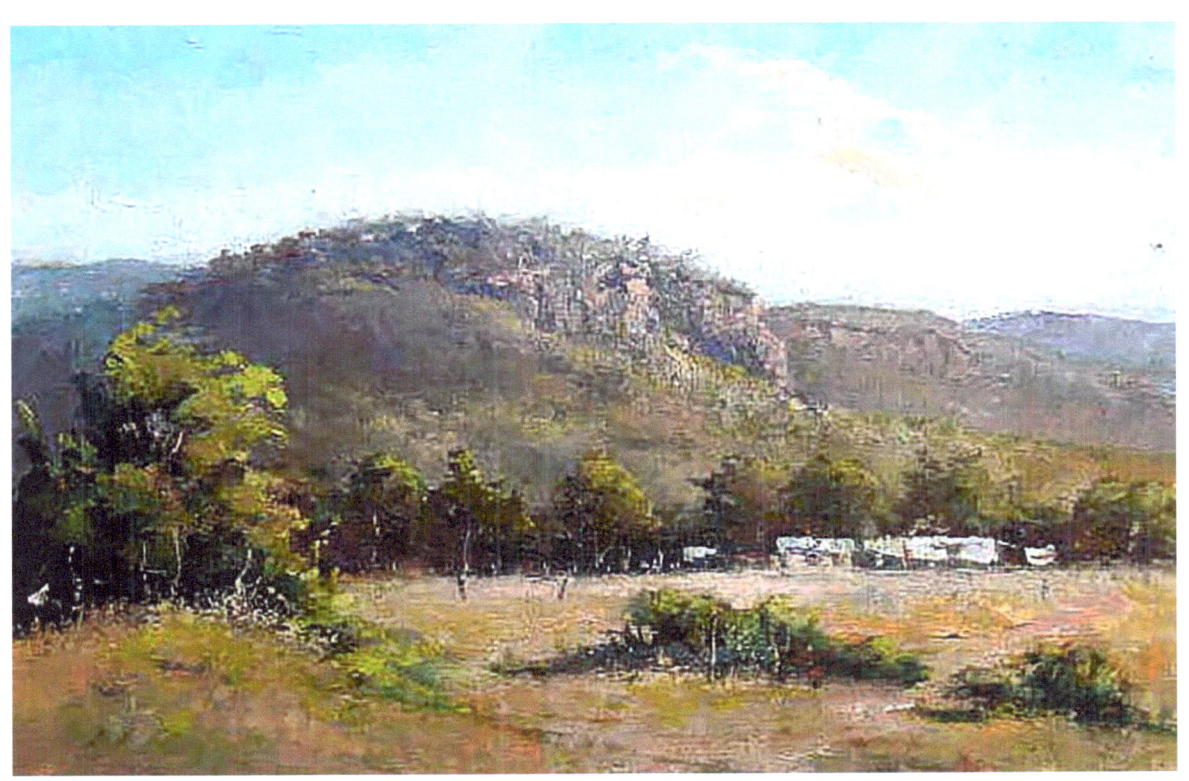

The Old Gum

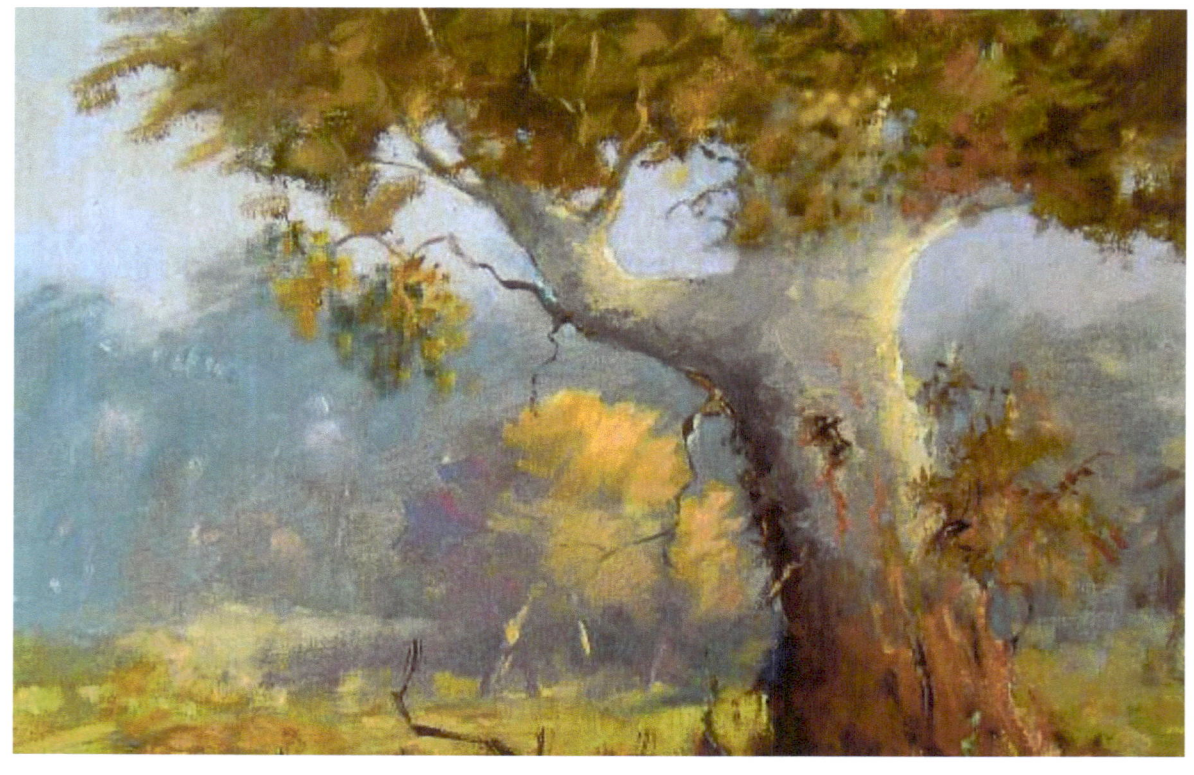

The Valley

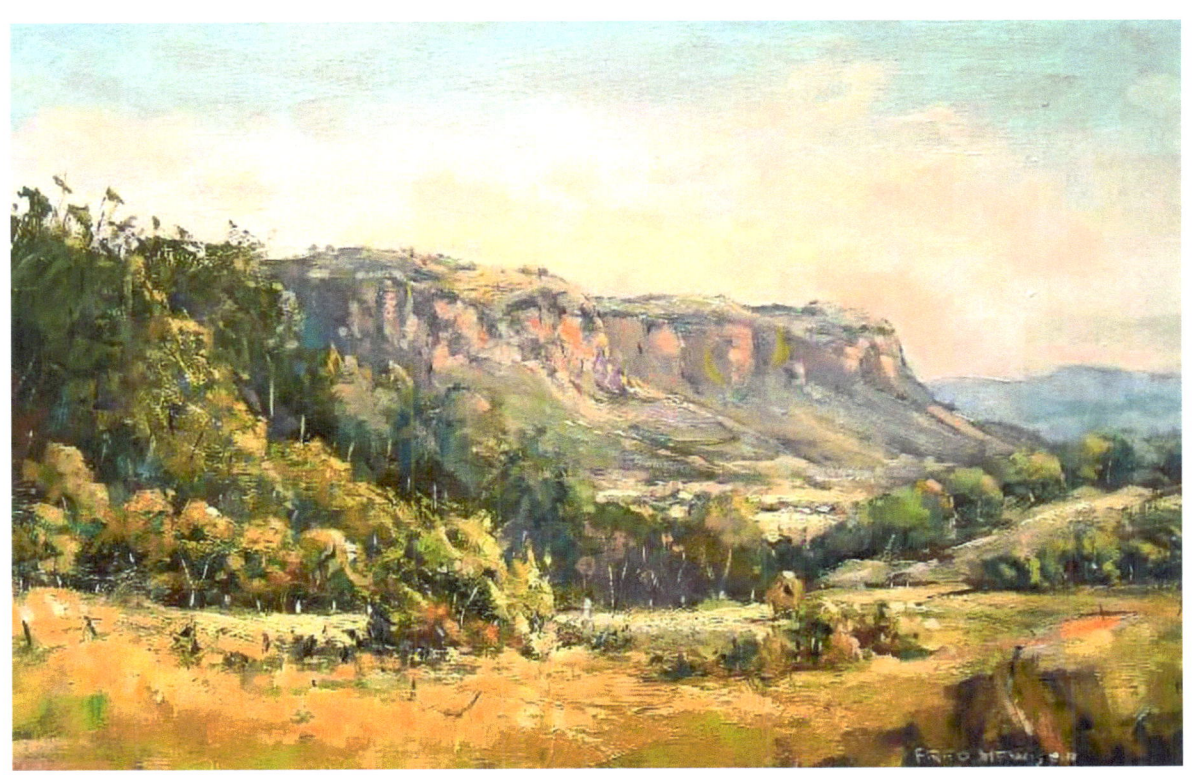

Tweed River, NSW

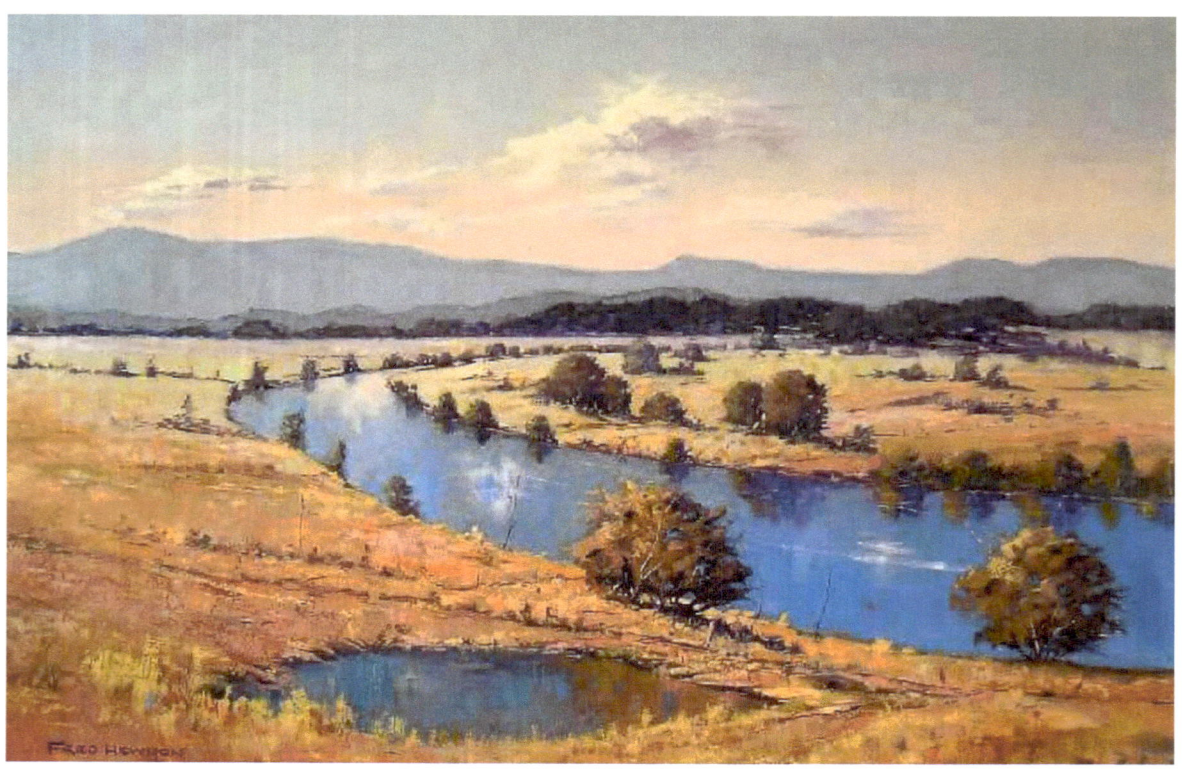

Tweed River, NSW

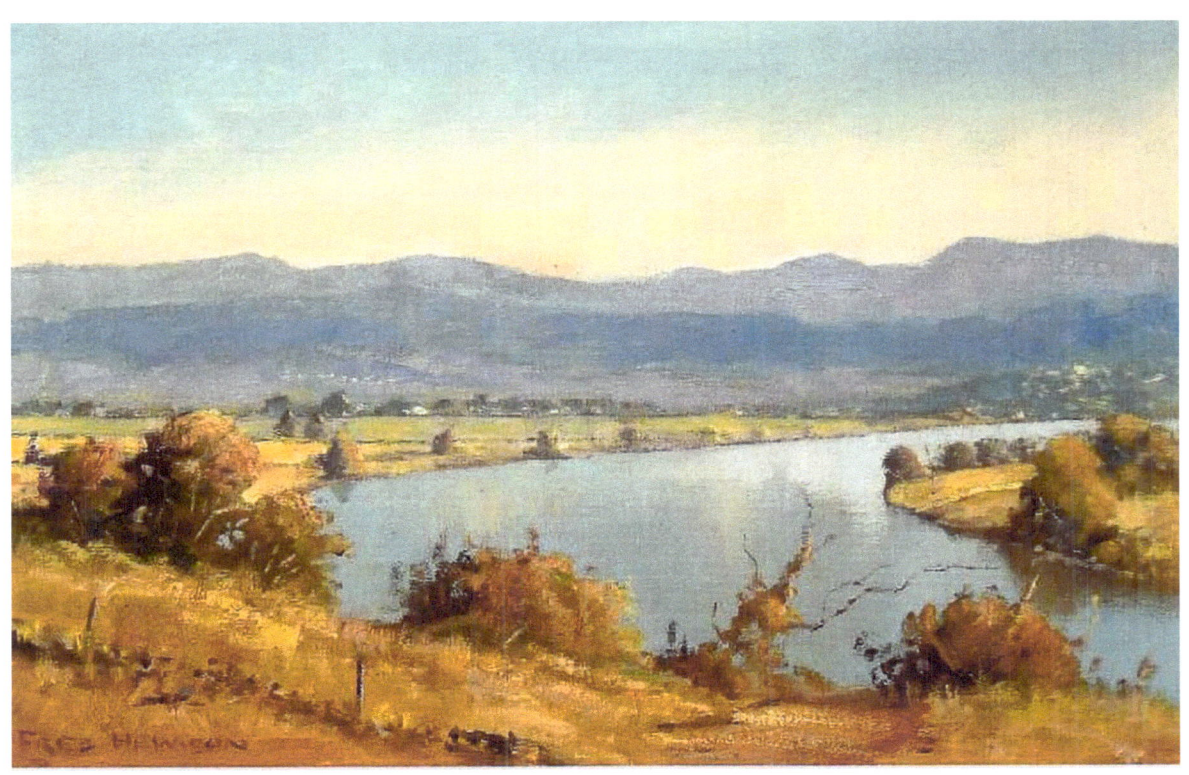

Mount Warning and The Tweed

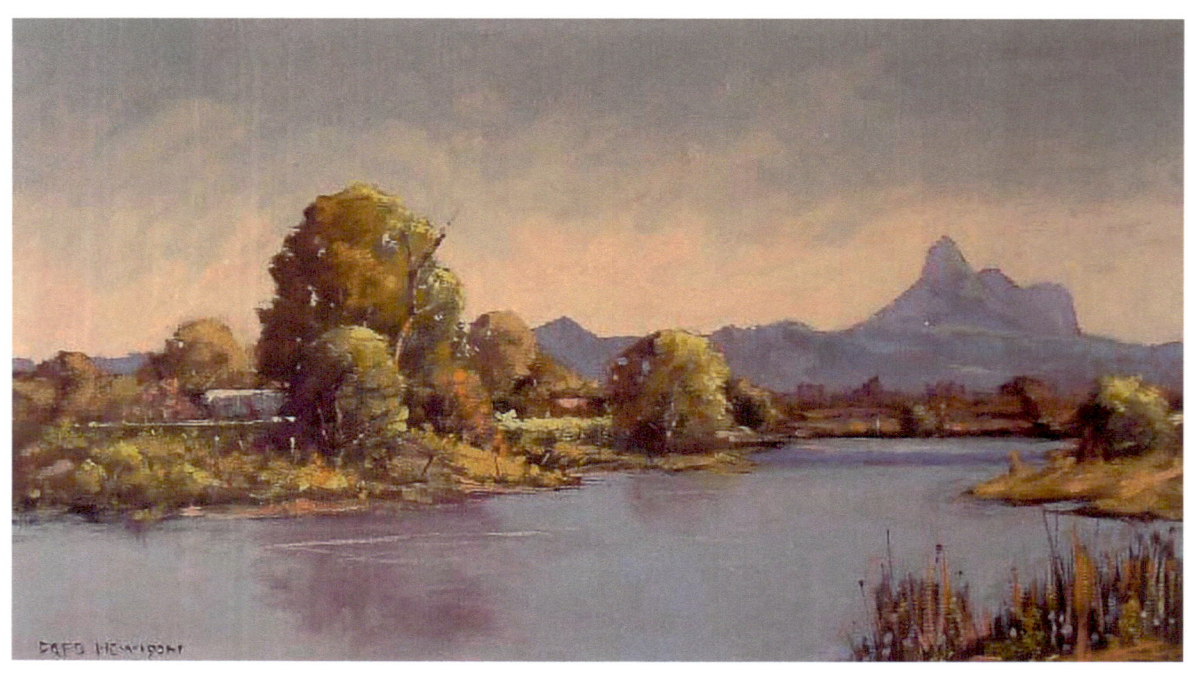

The Tweed from Bakers Road

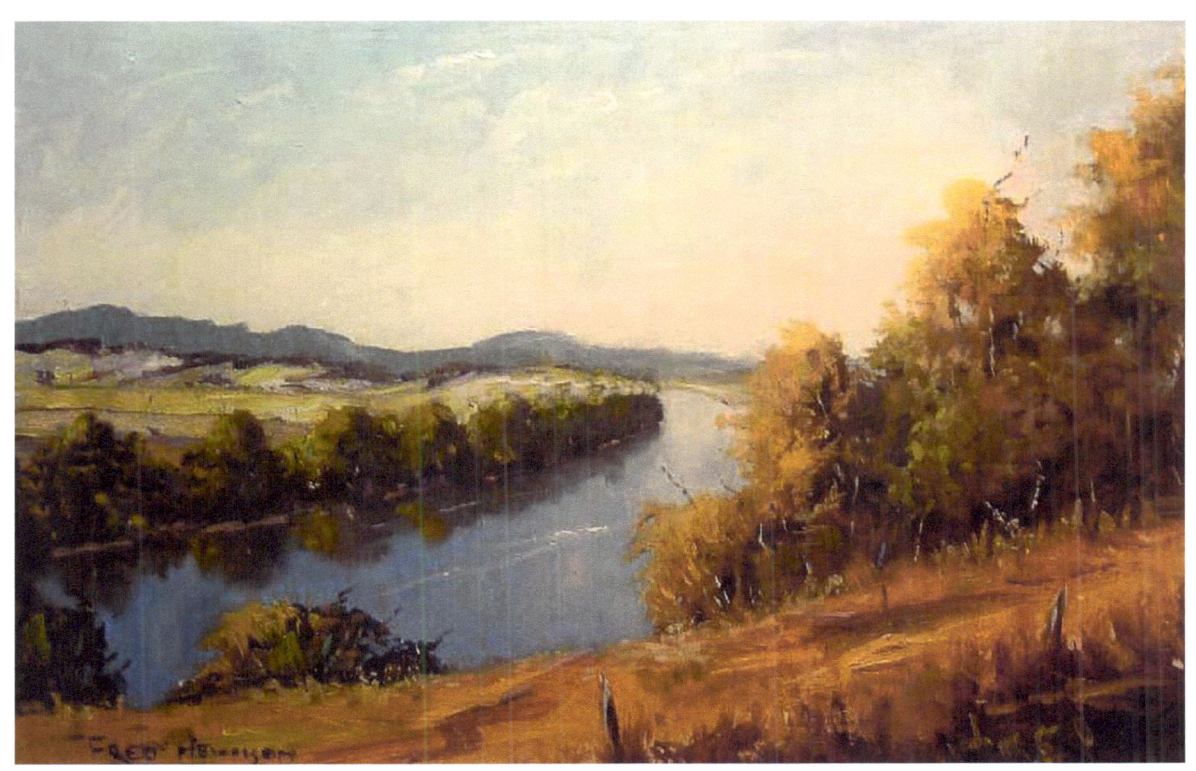

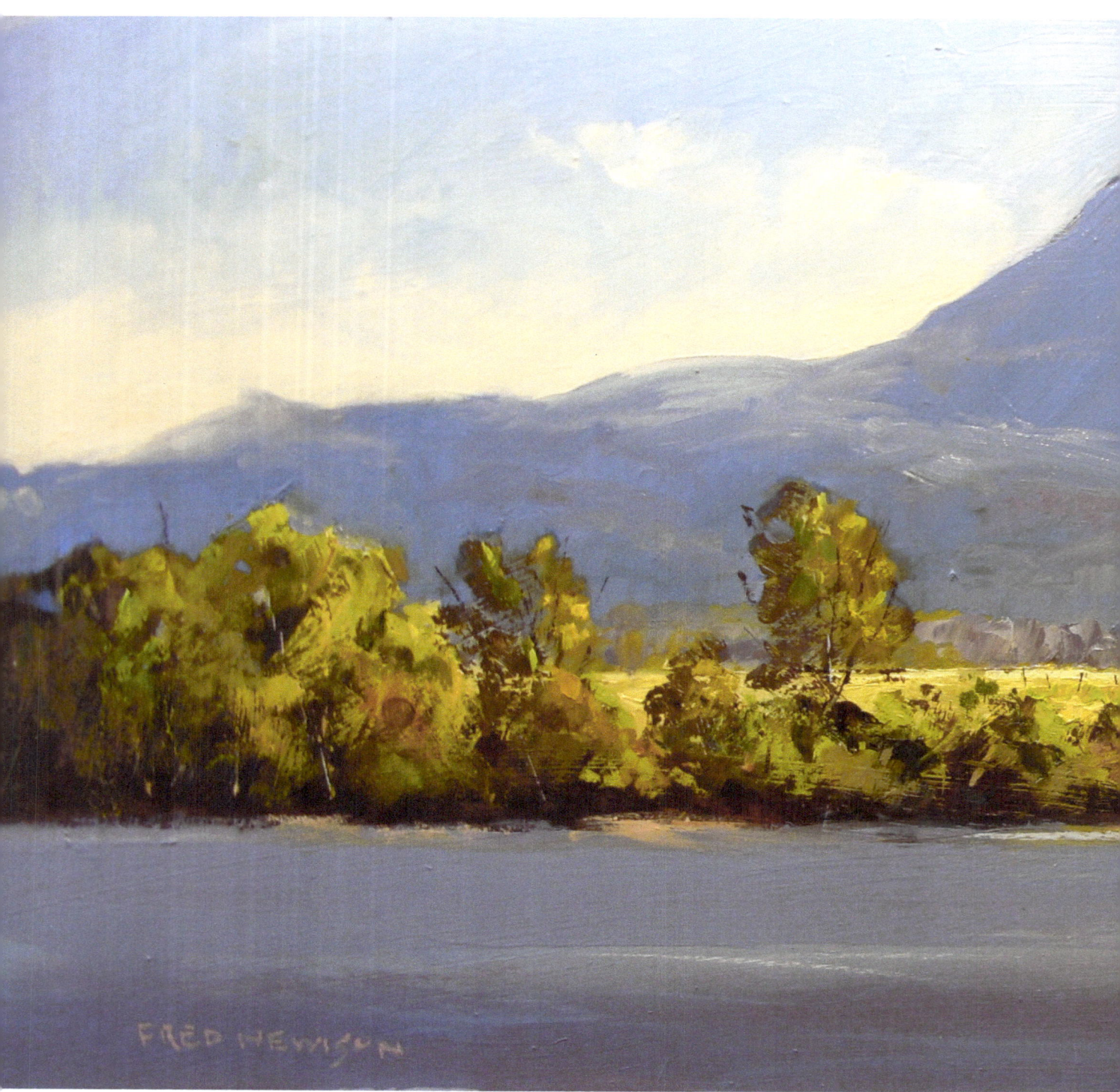

Tweed River, Tumbulgum

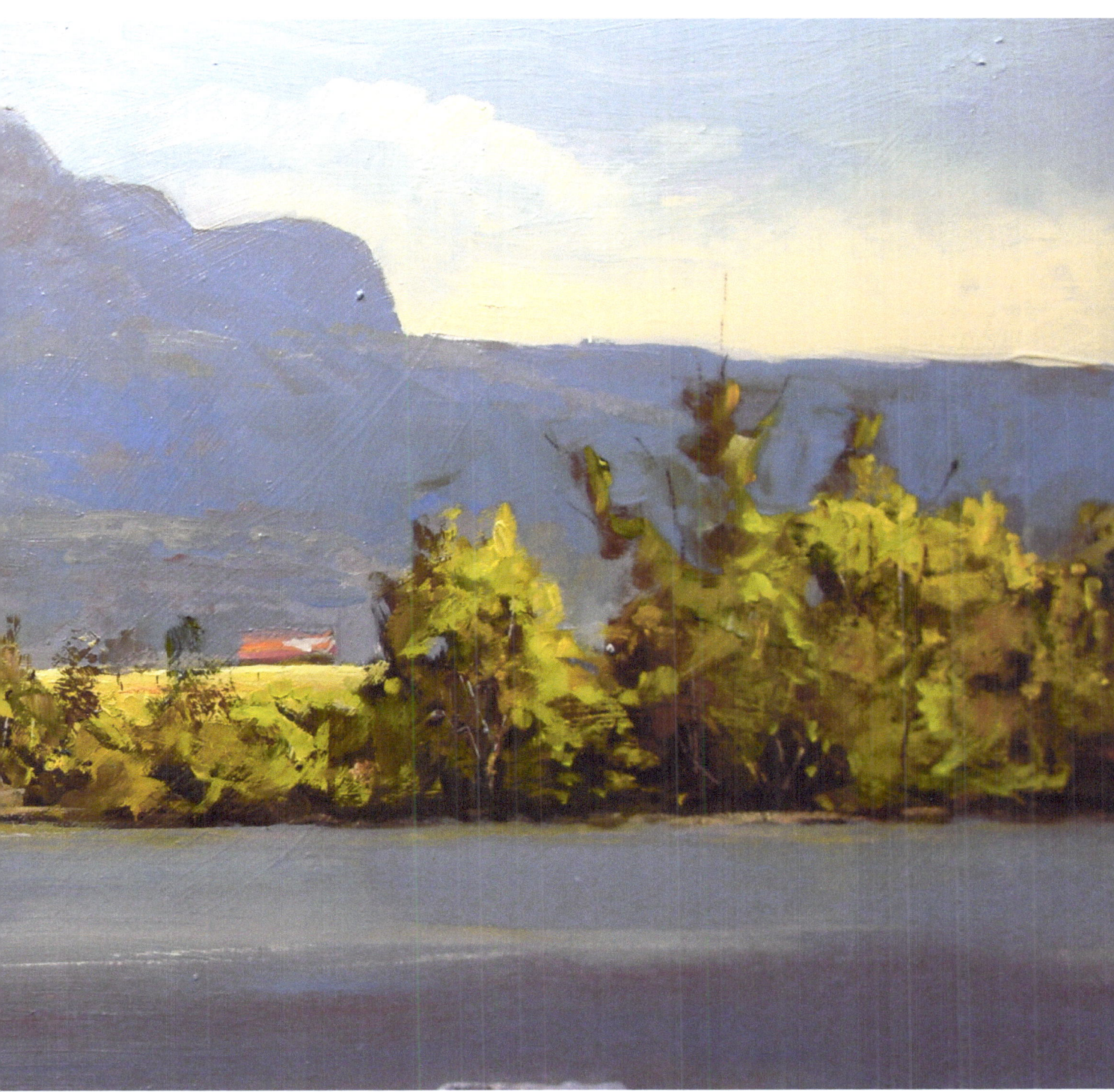

Creek Currumbin Valley, Queensland

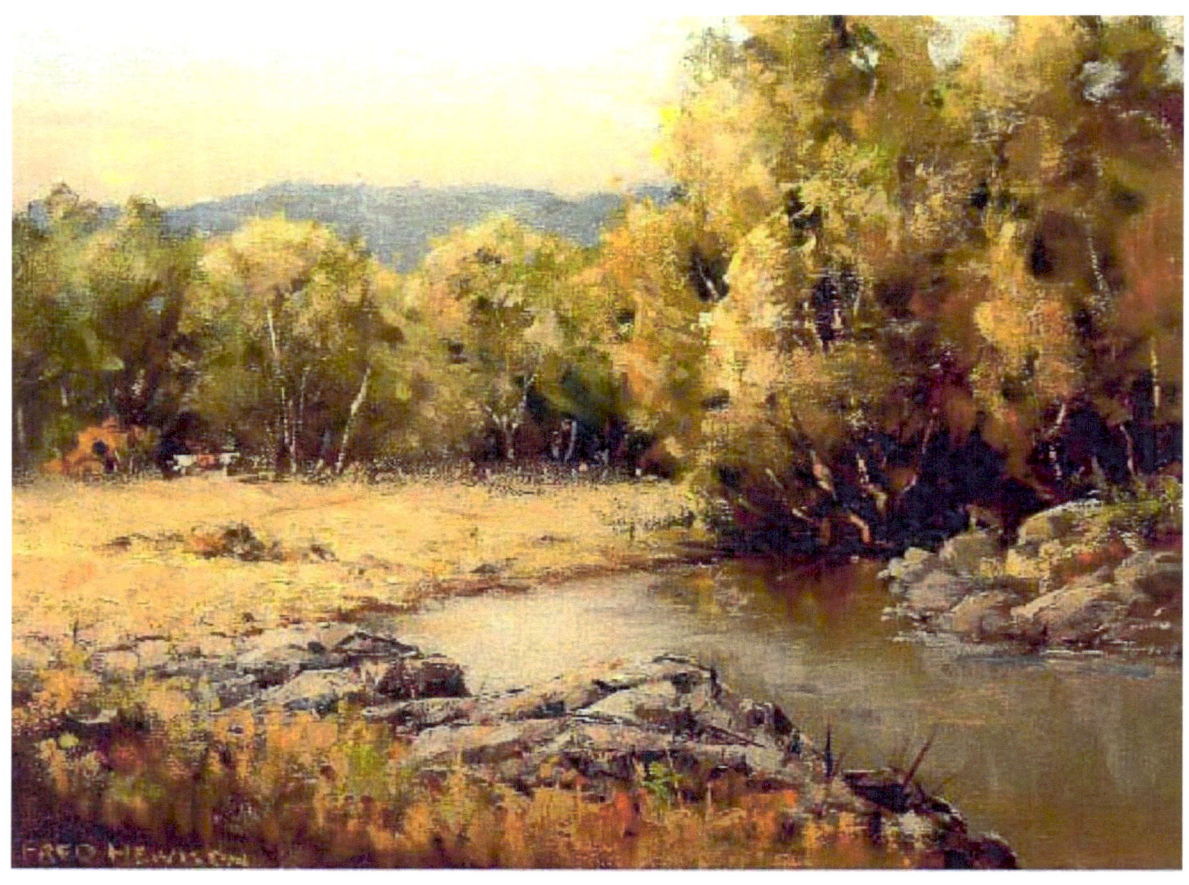

A Place to Rest

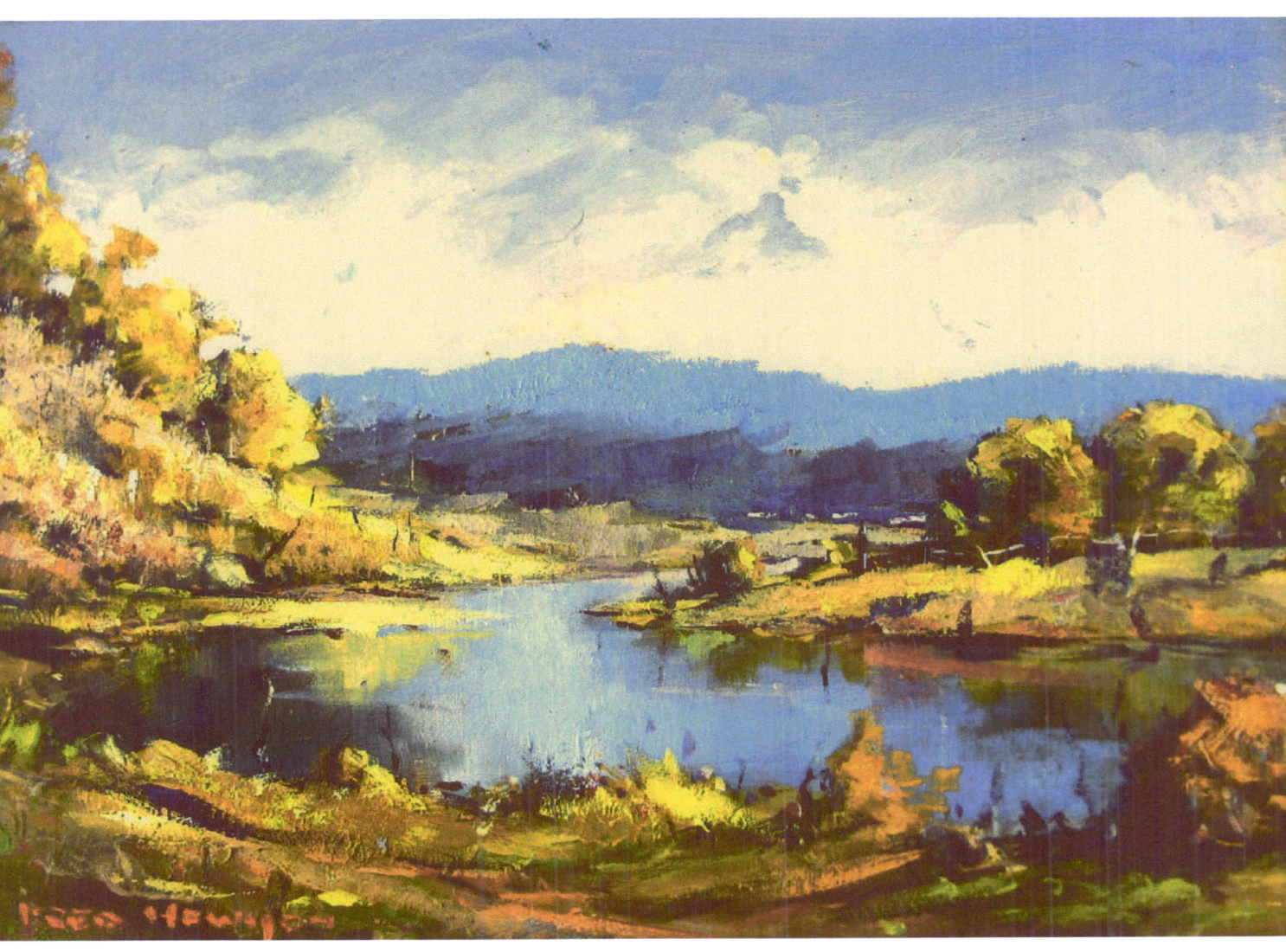

Terranora, NSW

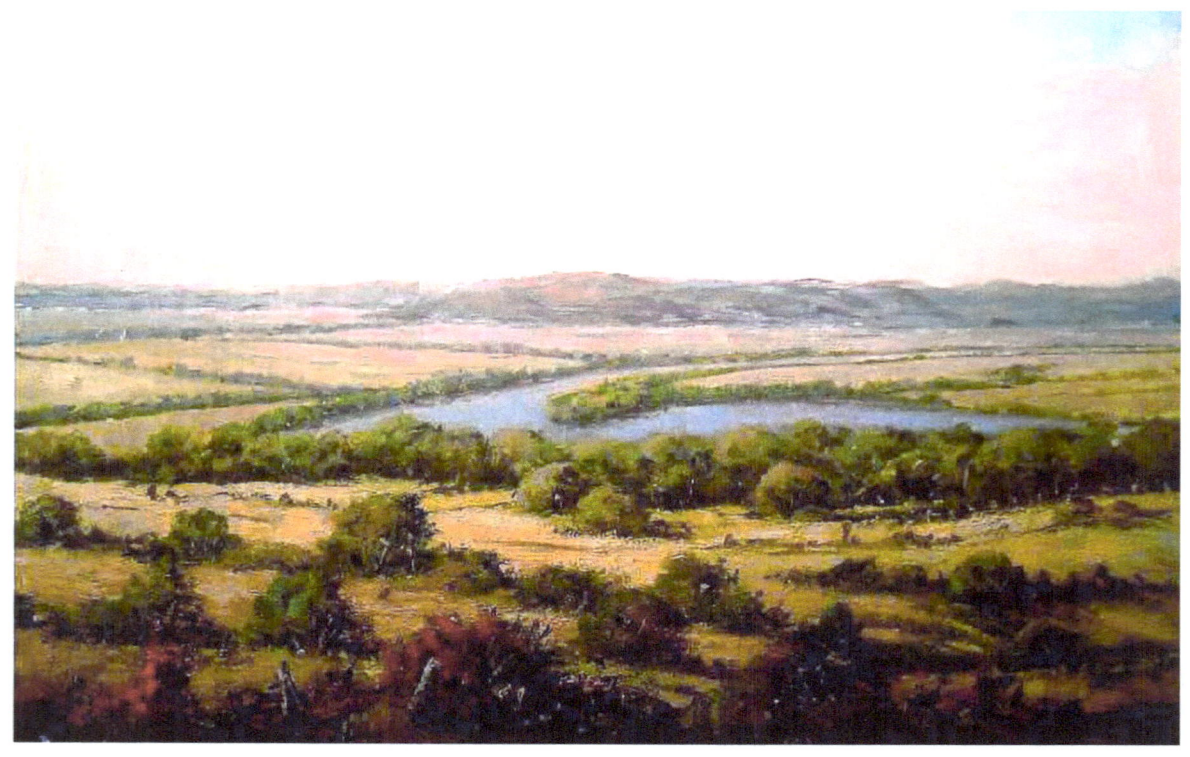

Hastings Point, NSW

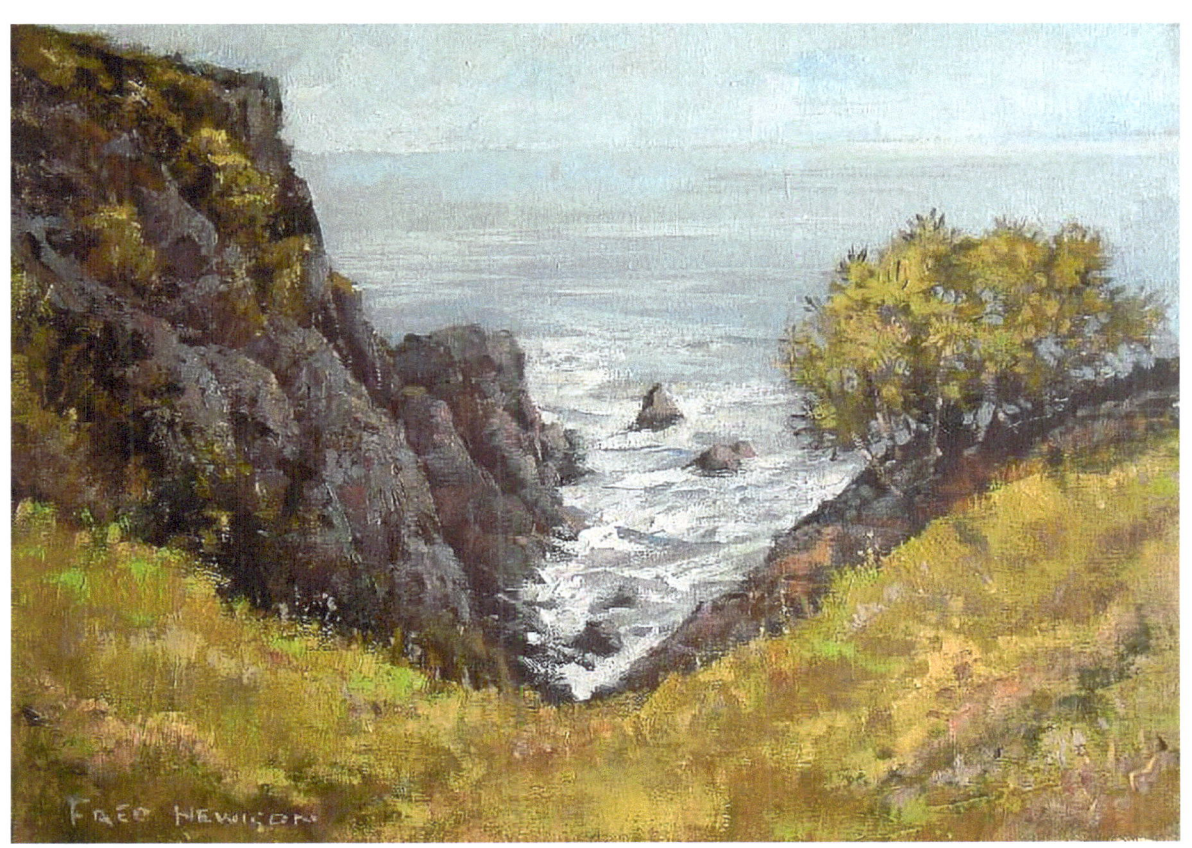

Murwllumbah–Uki Crossing

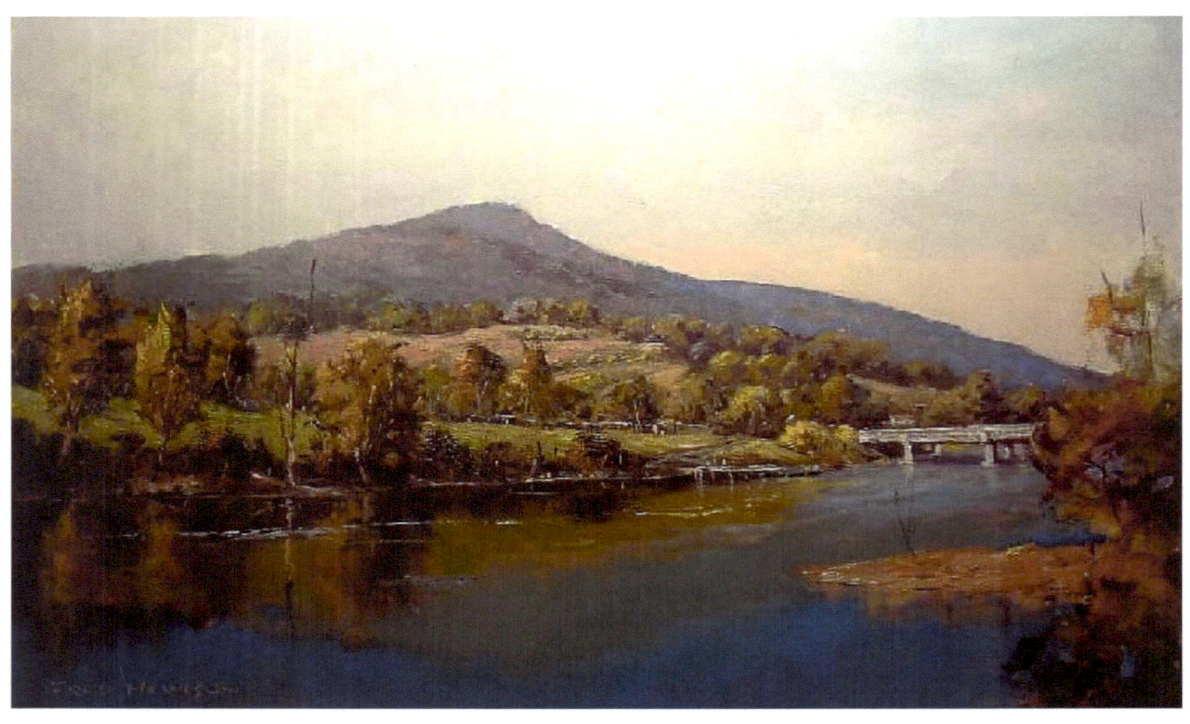

Kangaroo Creek, NSW

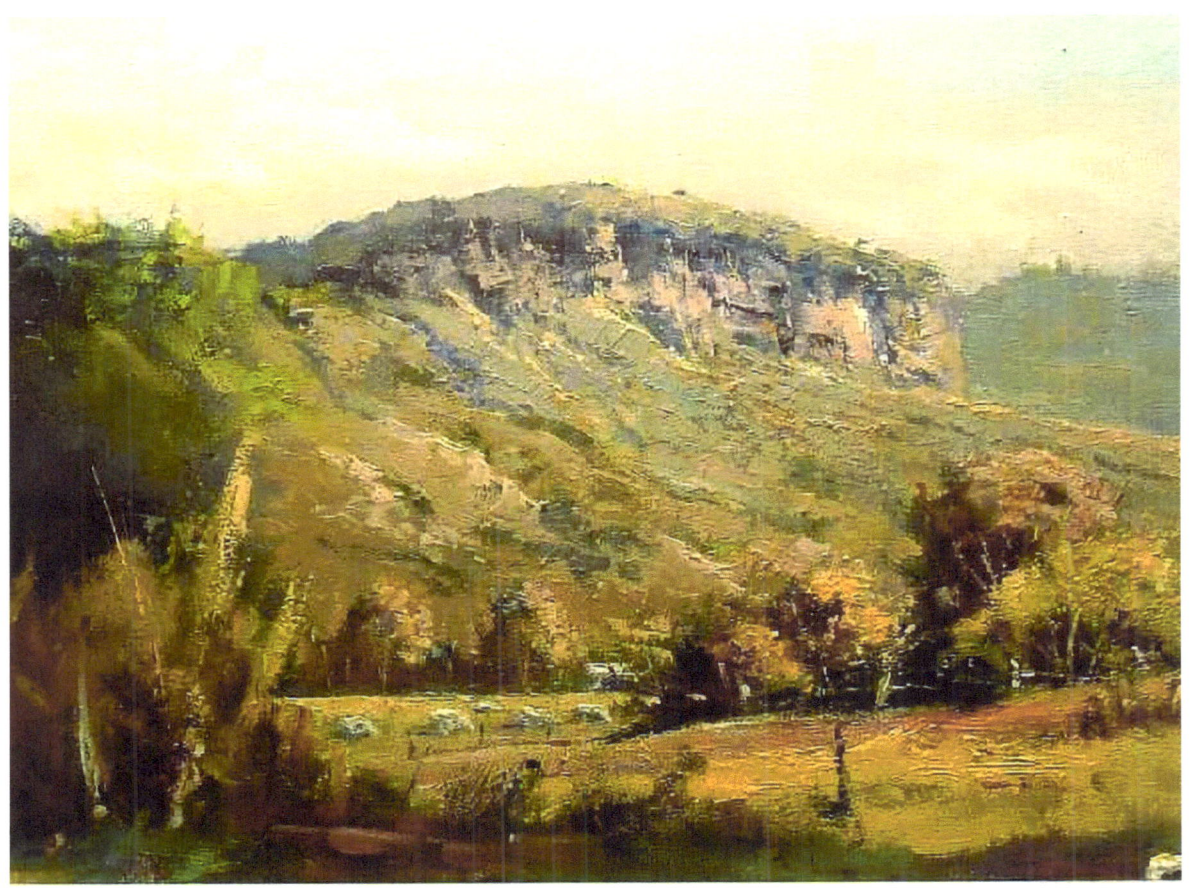

Timor Rock, Coonabarrabran

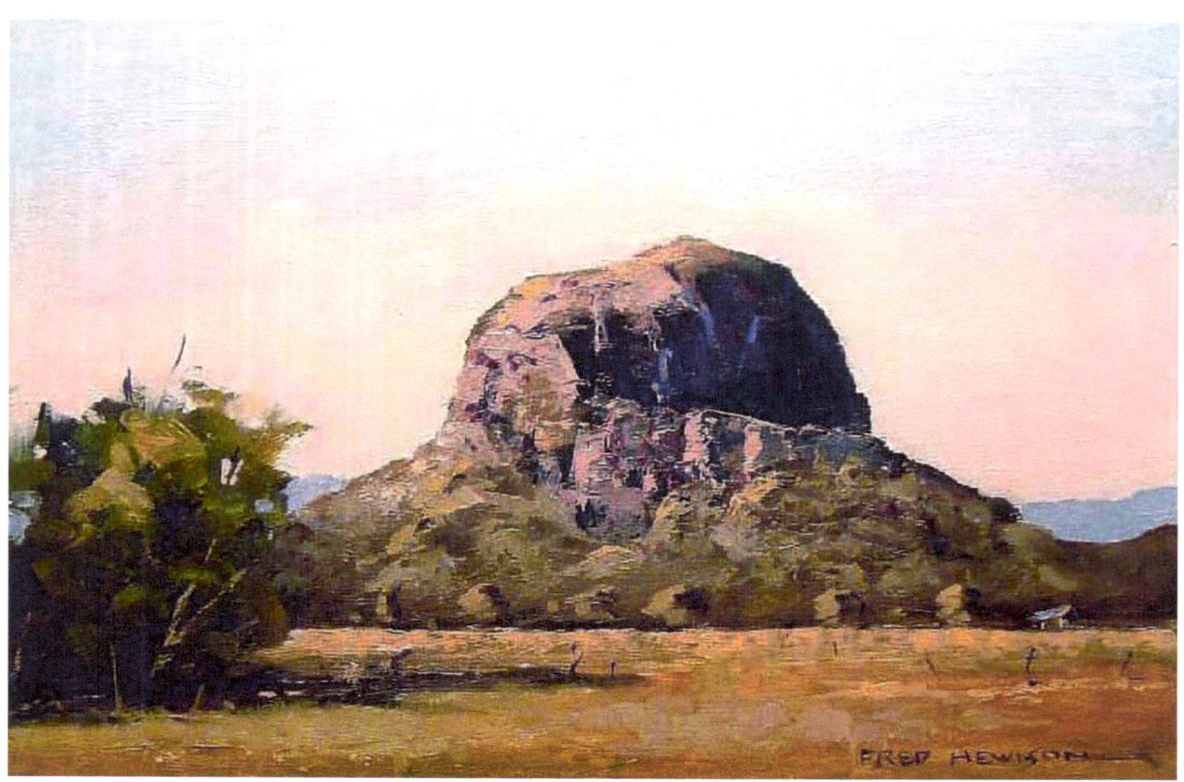

Australia Vast

LANDSCAPES IN OILS

The Gouldburn River, Victoria

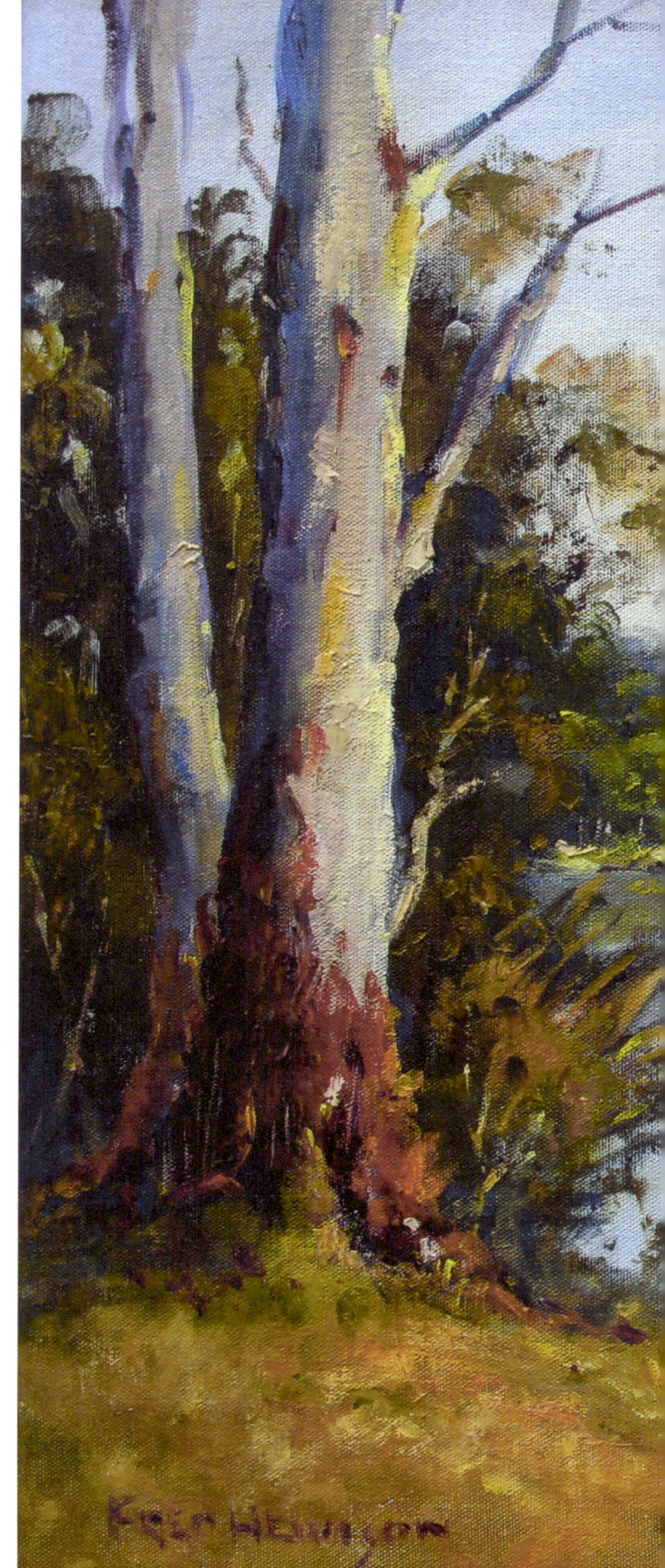

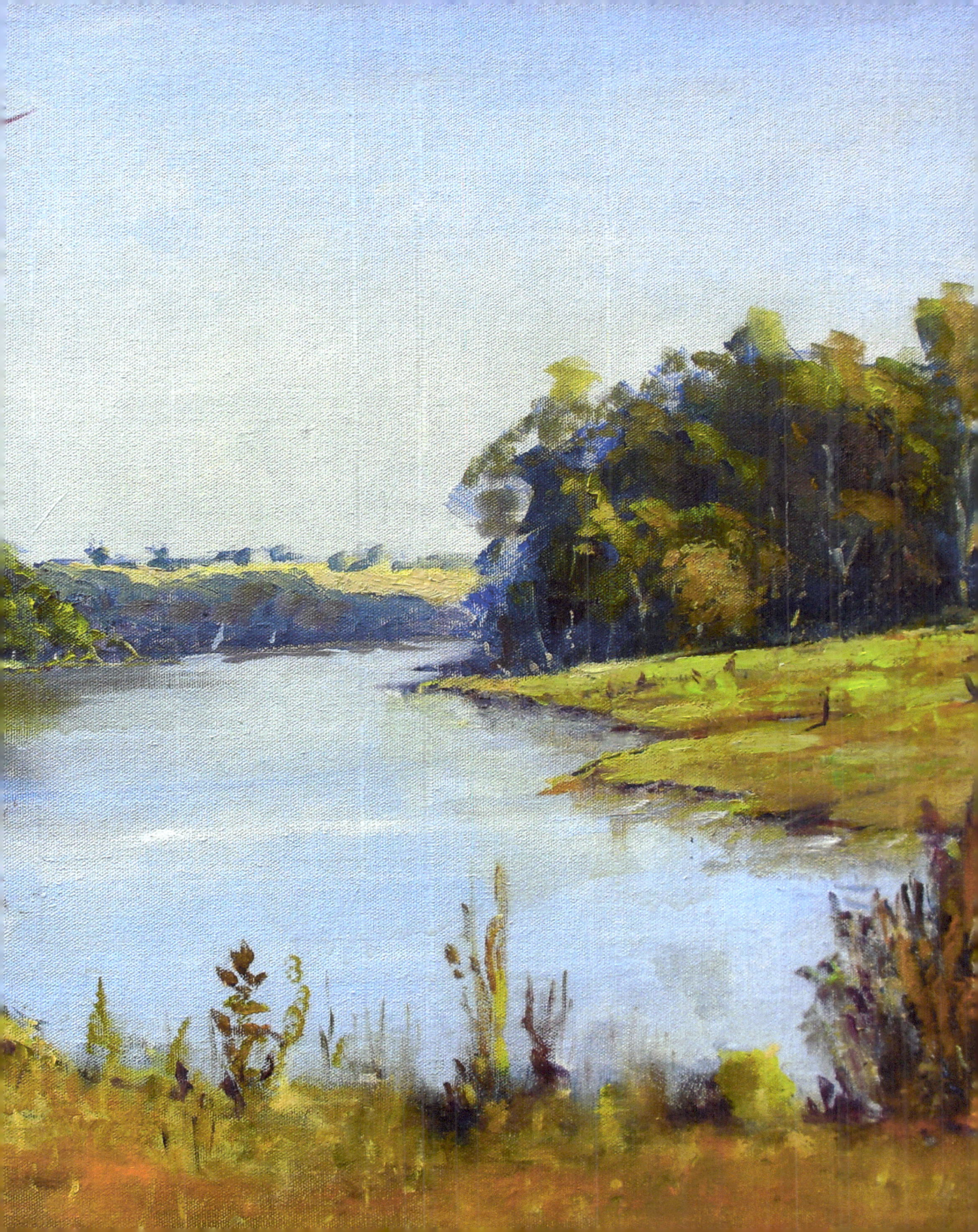

Doon Donn Via Uki, NSW

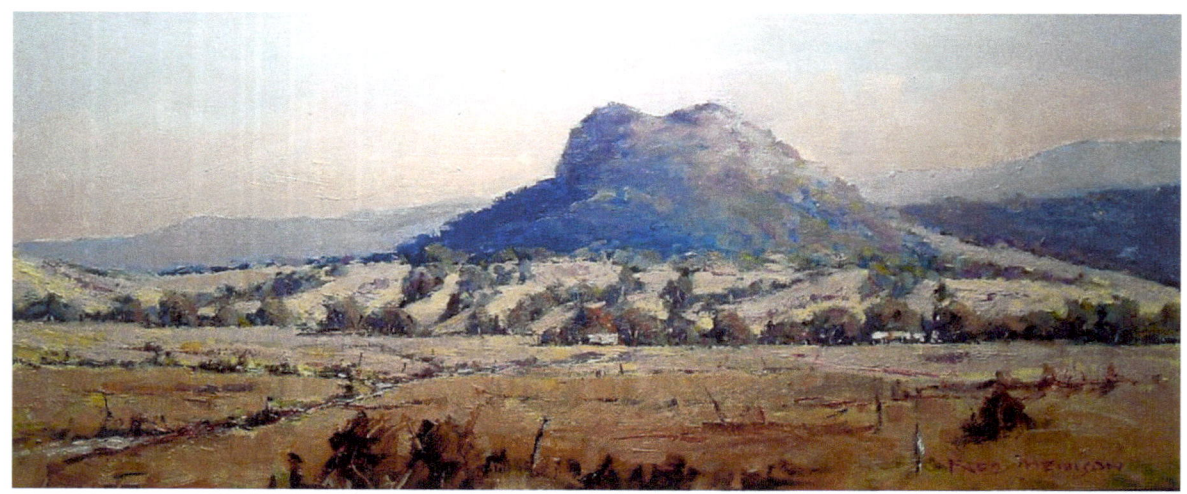

Upper Wilson

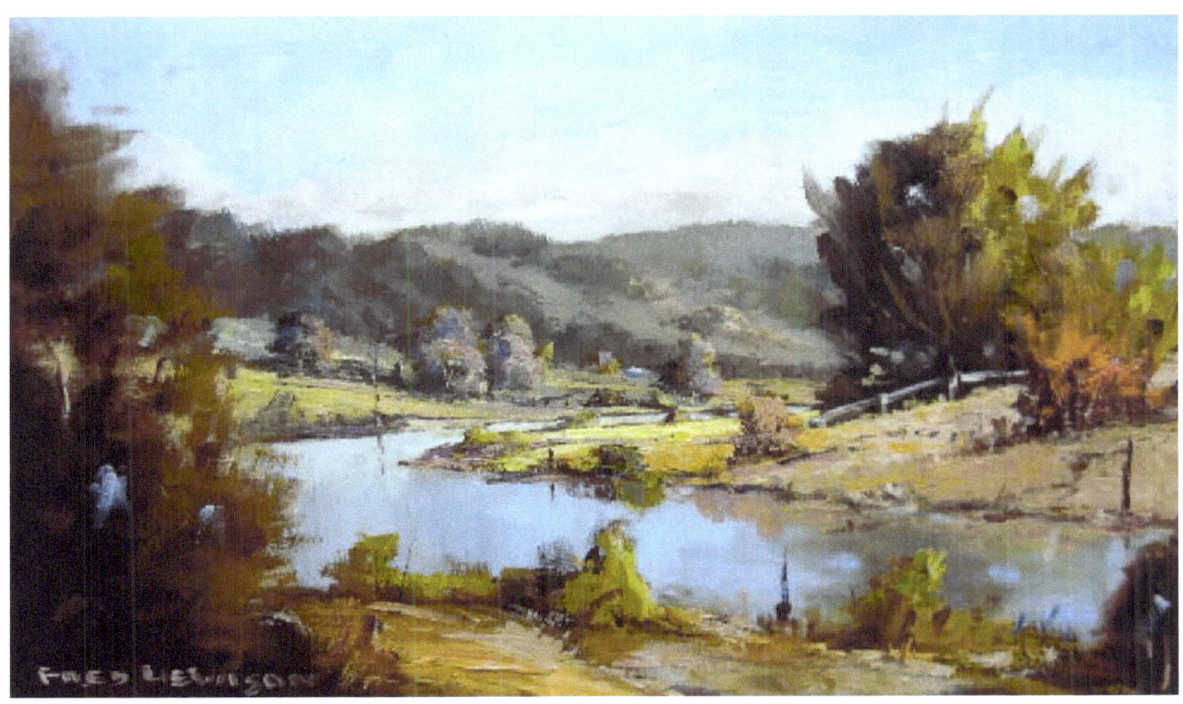

Hasting Point, NSW

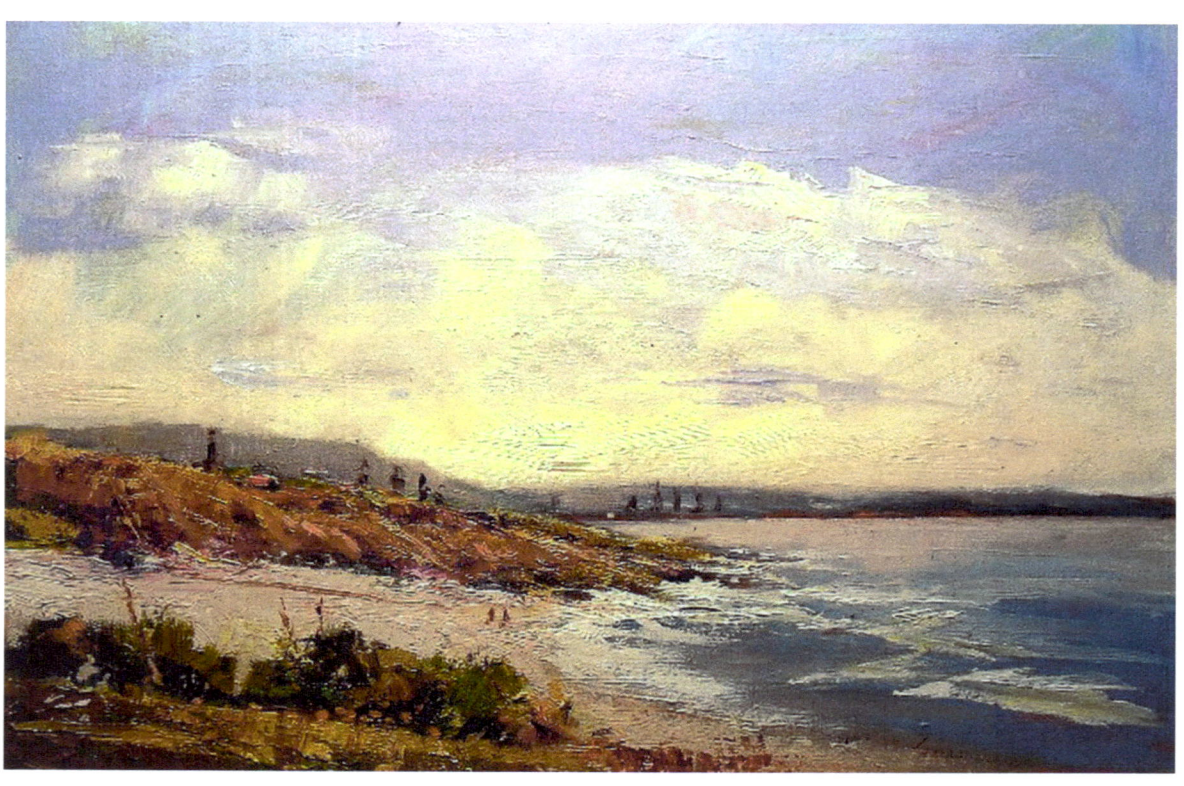

Upper Rous

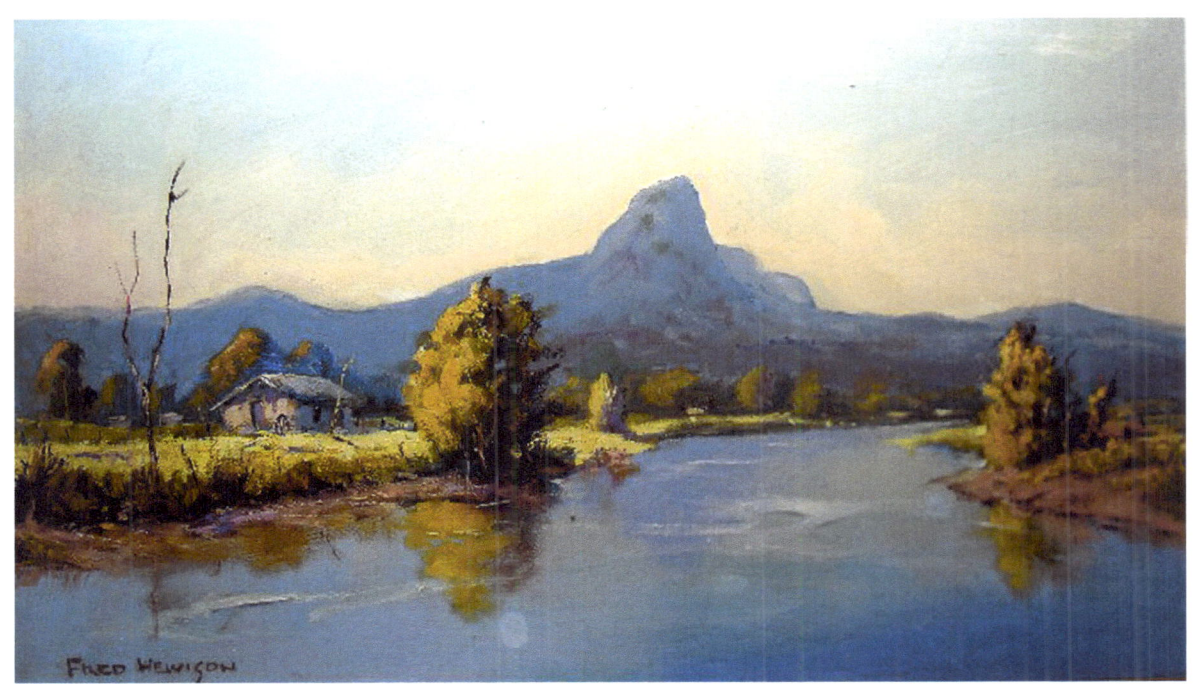

Creative

Upper Rous (2)

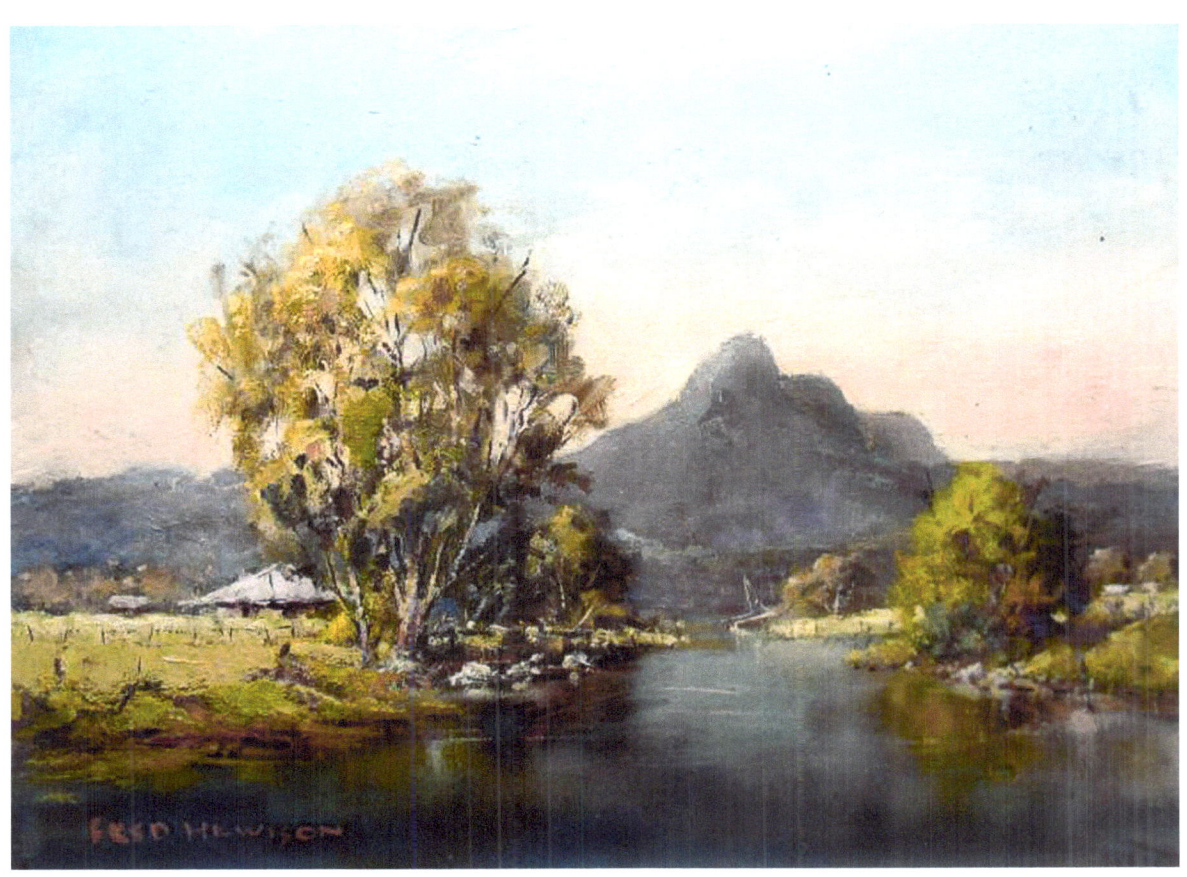

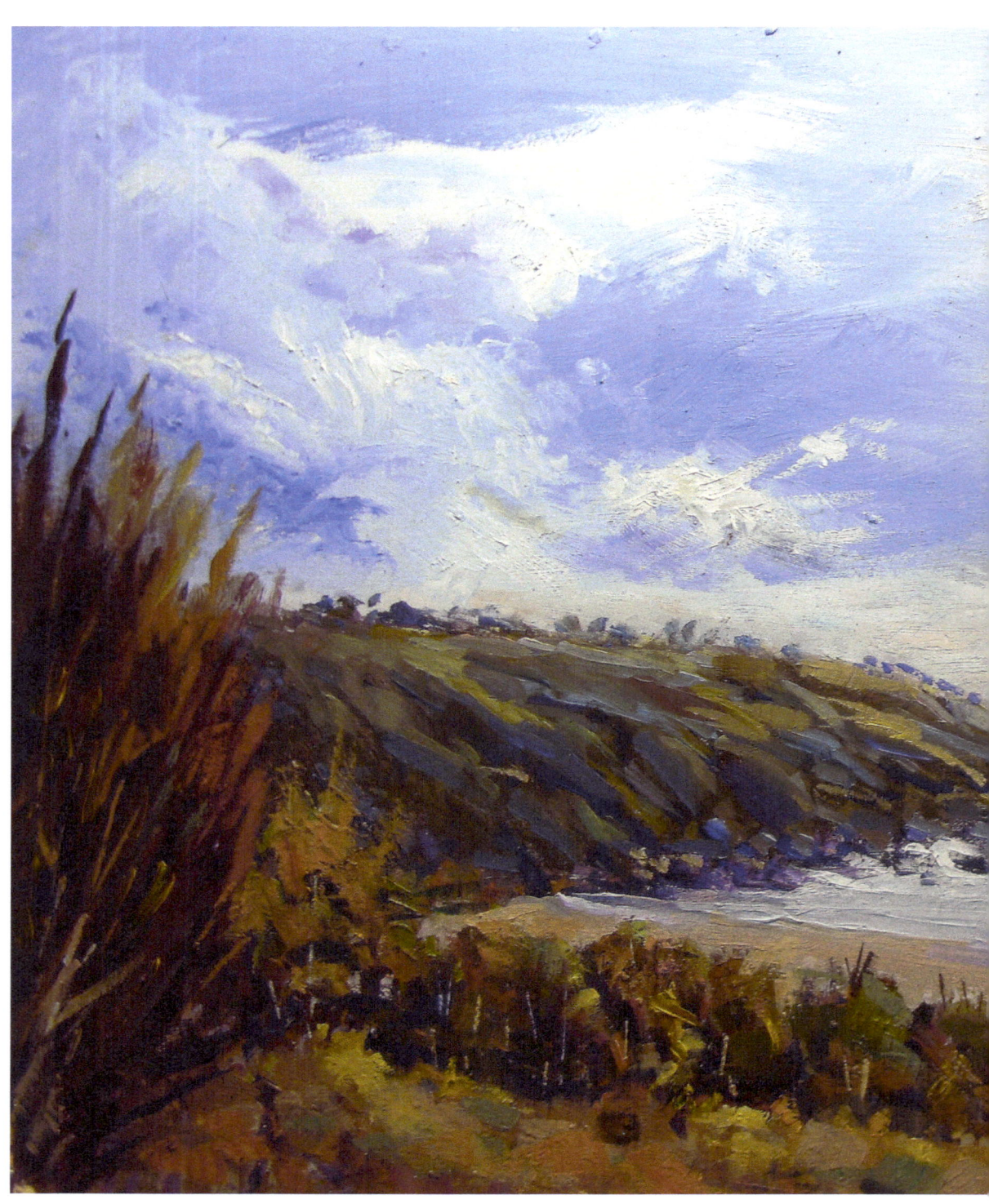

Arrawarra Headland, NSW

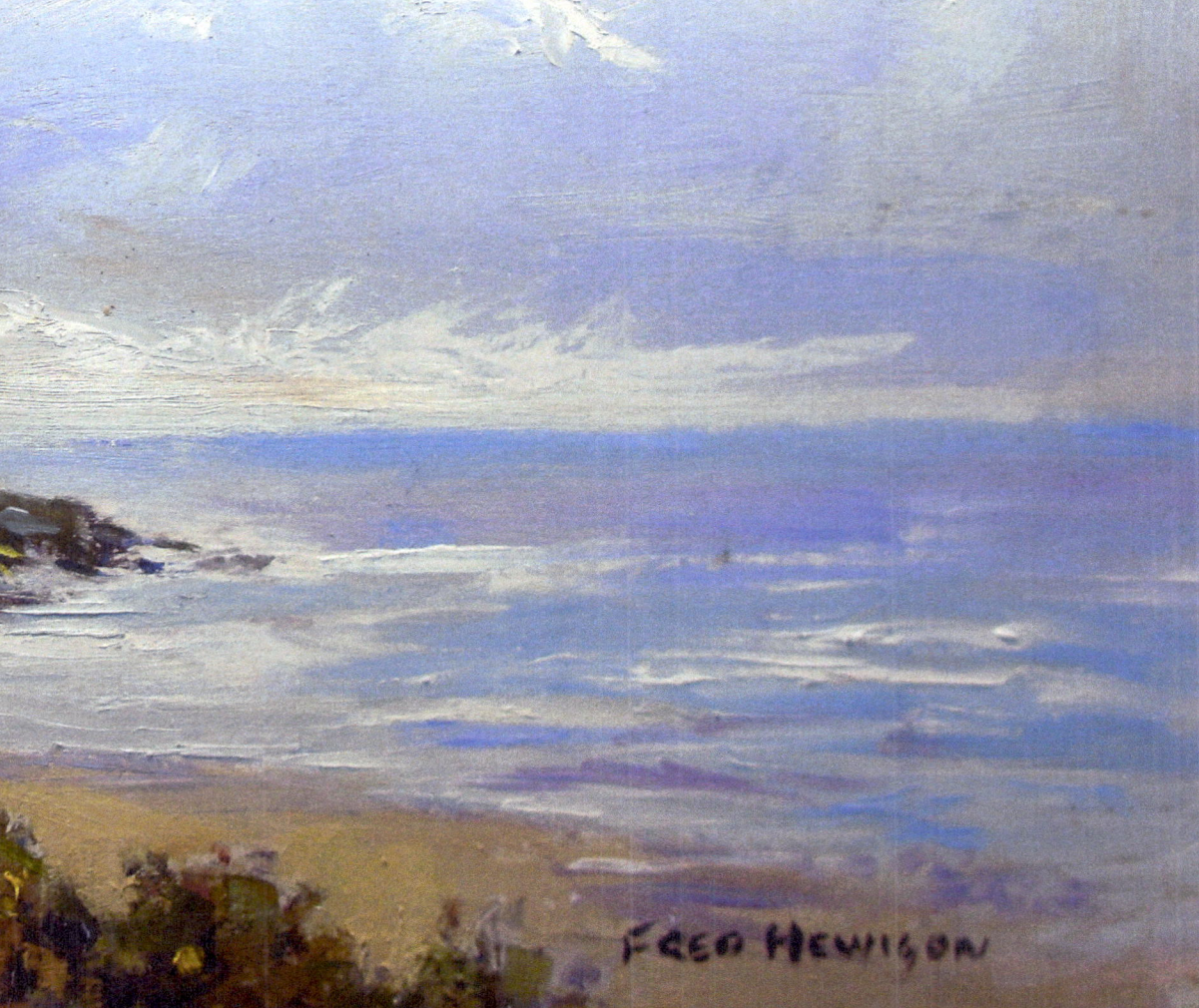

The Beautiful Tweed

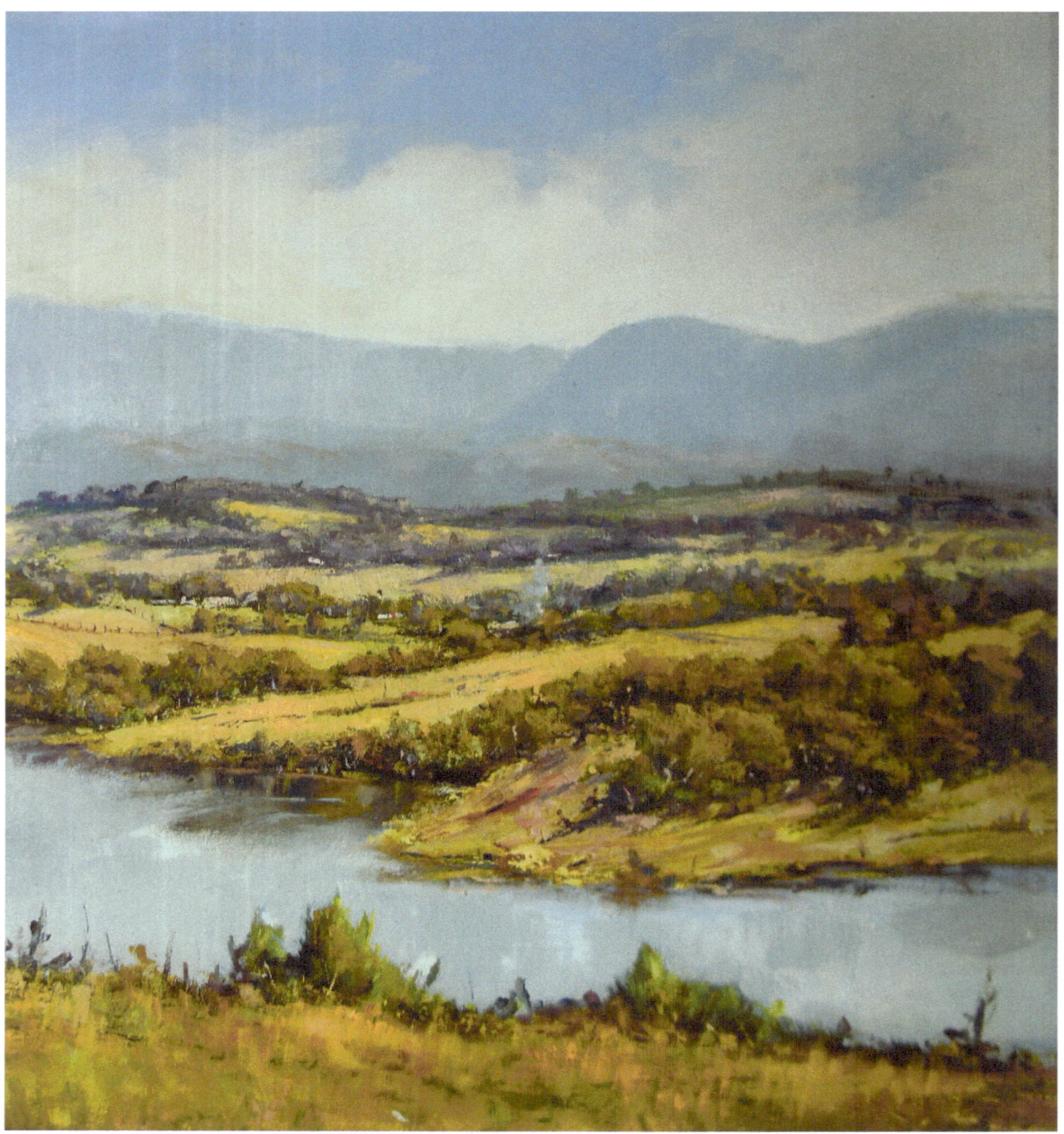

Across The Bay

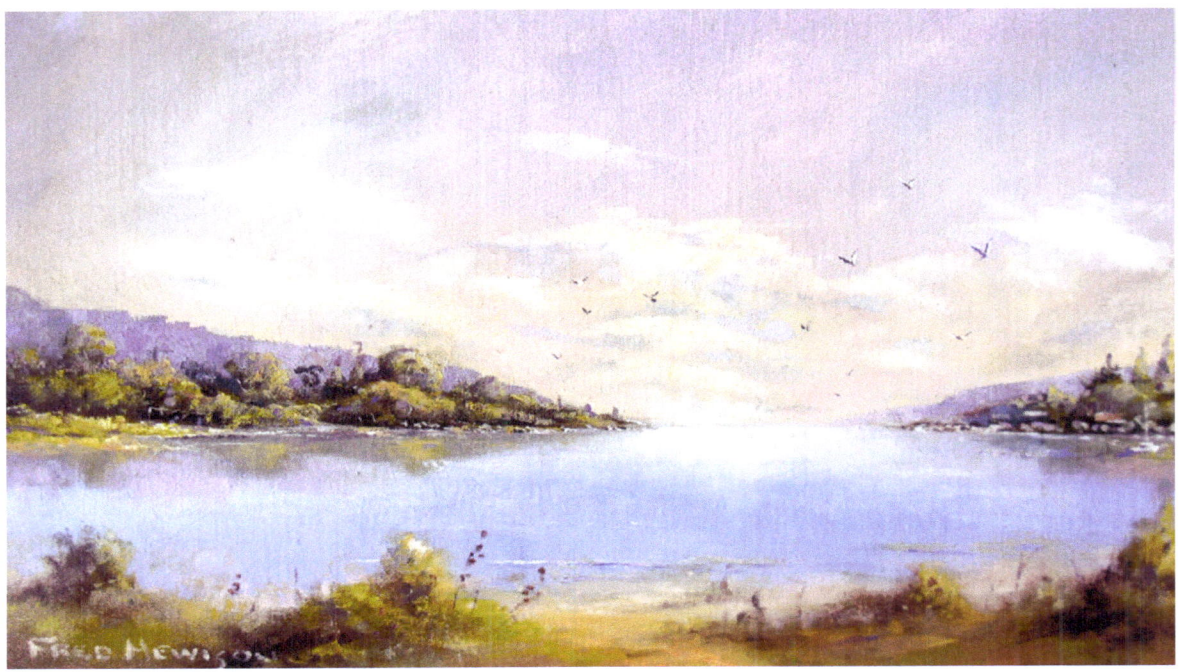

A Quiet Place

The Old Farm

Pastures, Inverell, NSW

Duroby Creek

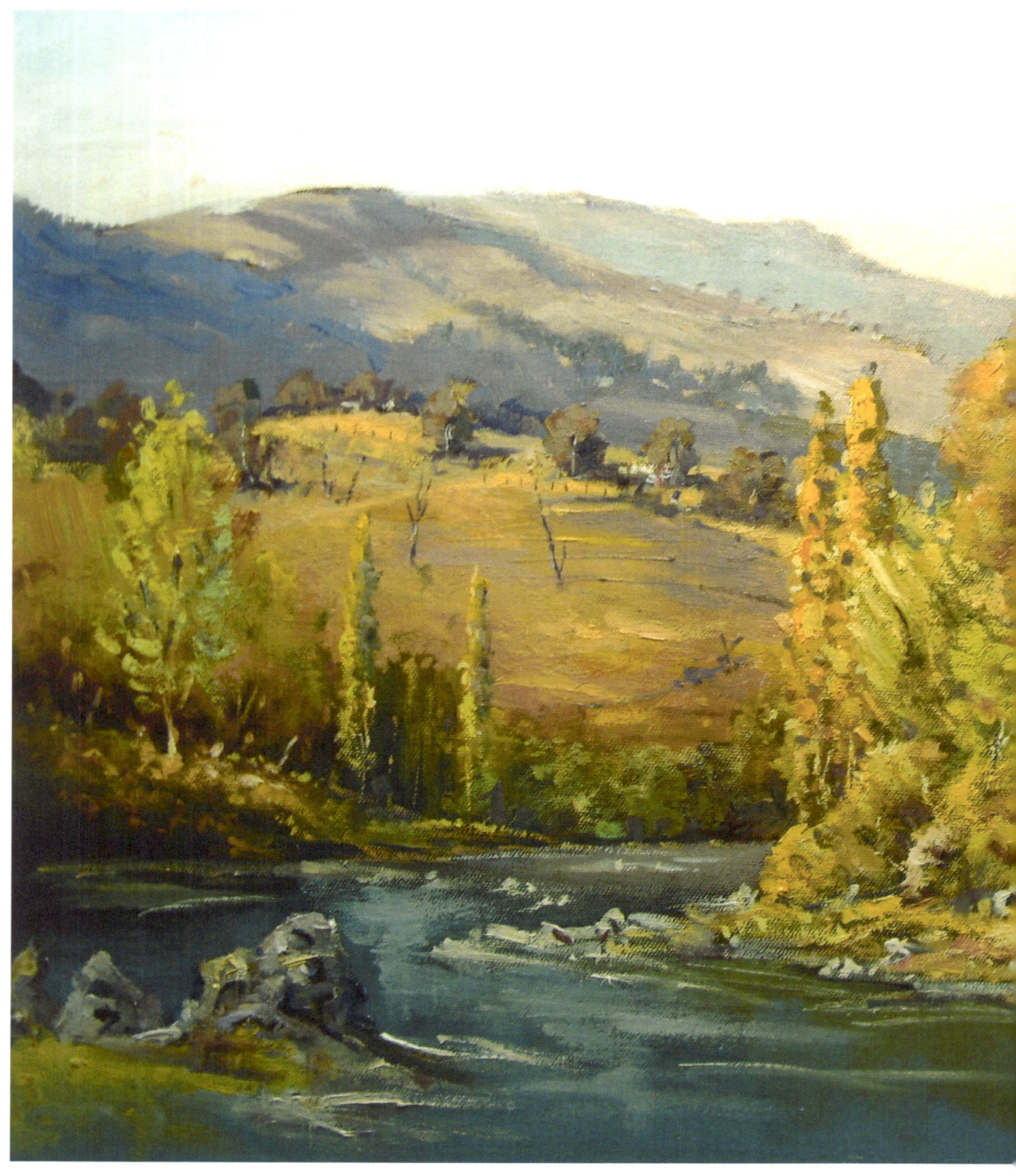

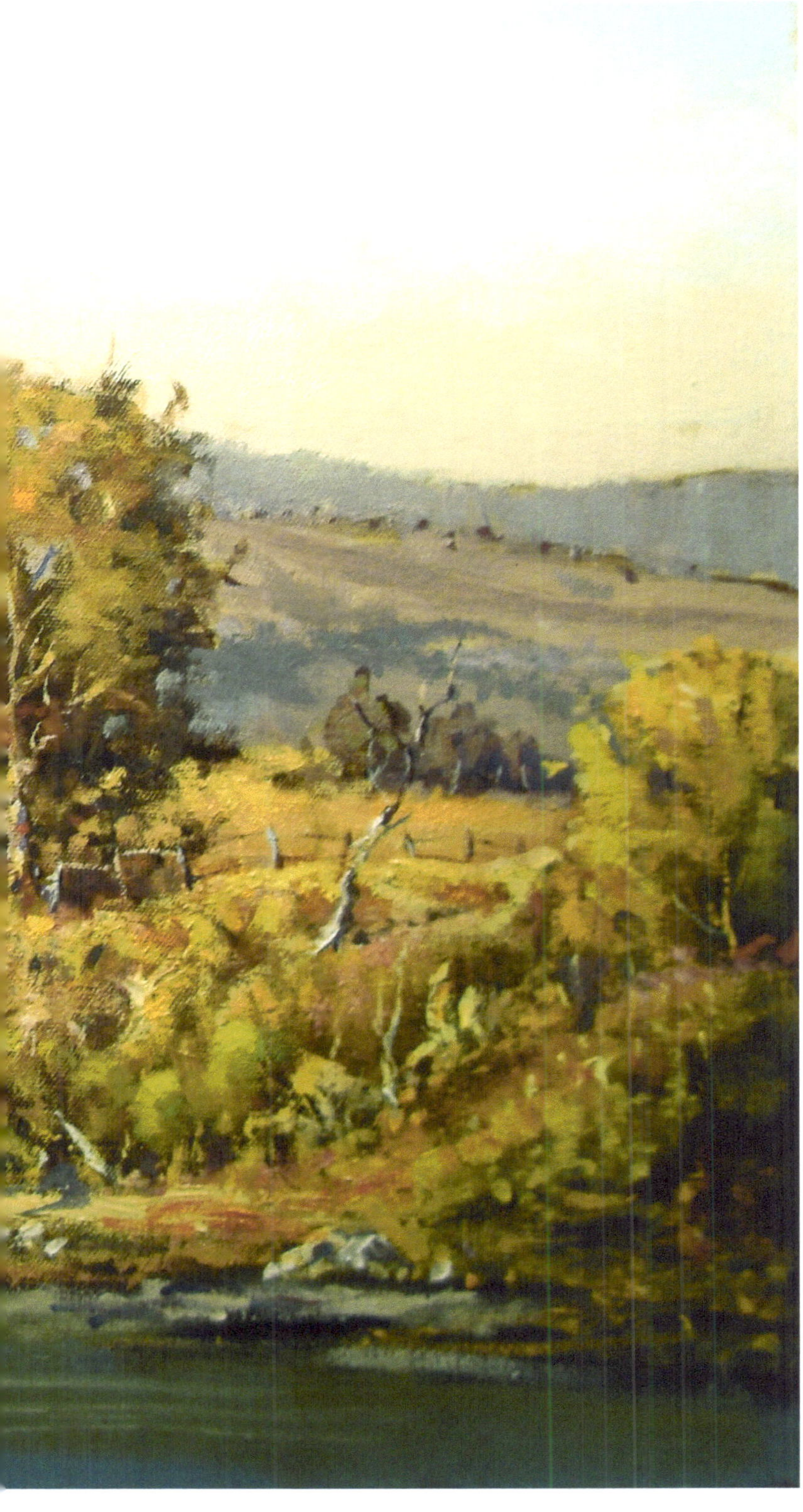

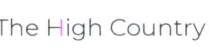
The High Country

The Little House

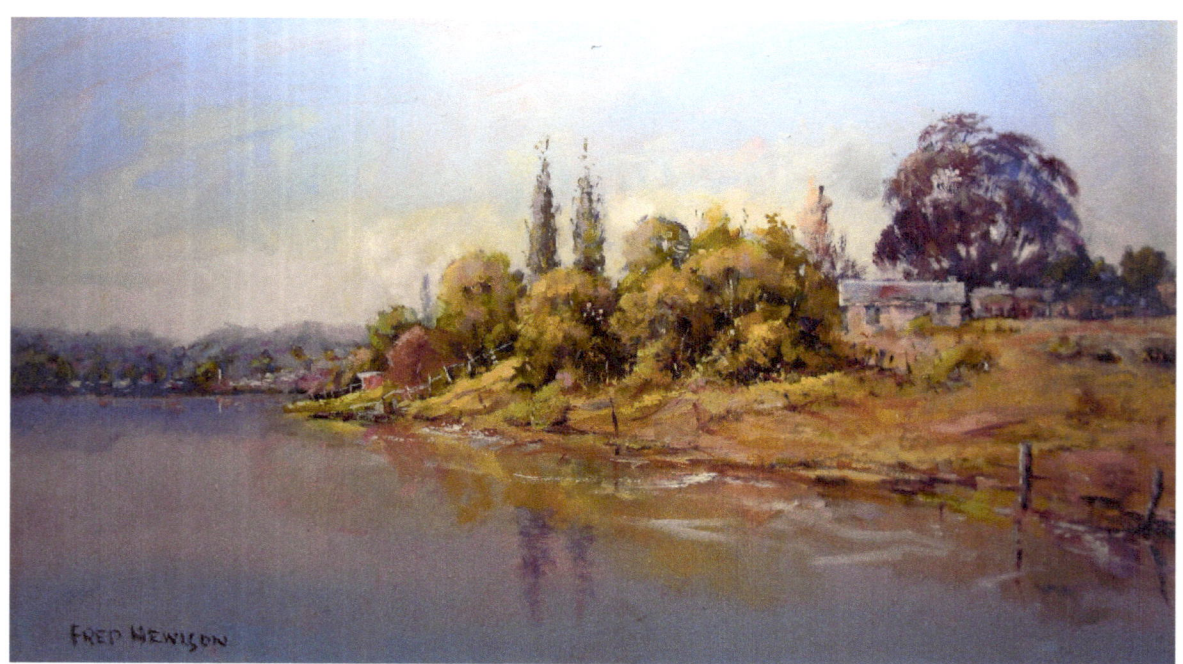

Edge of The Creek

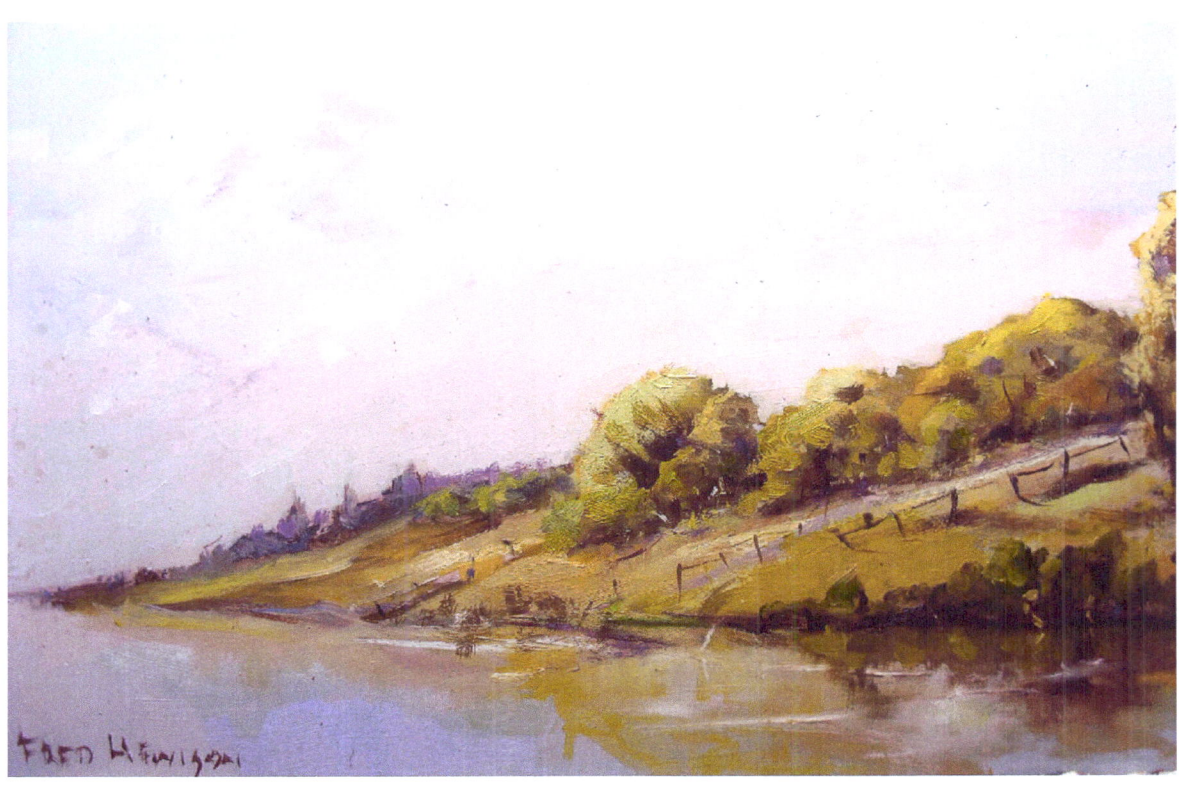

Near Stokers Siding

Towards Mount Warning

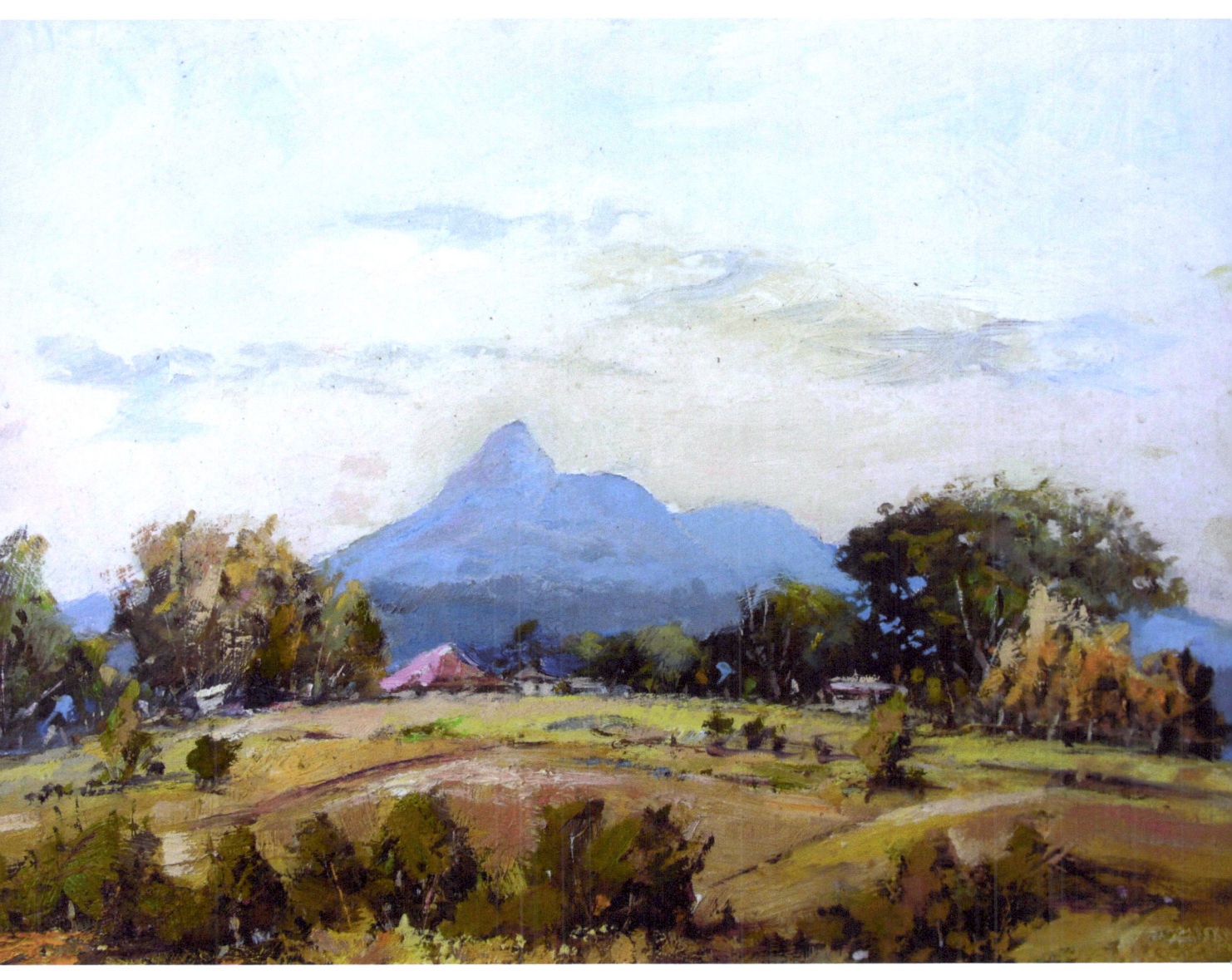

River Gum

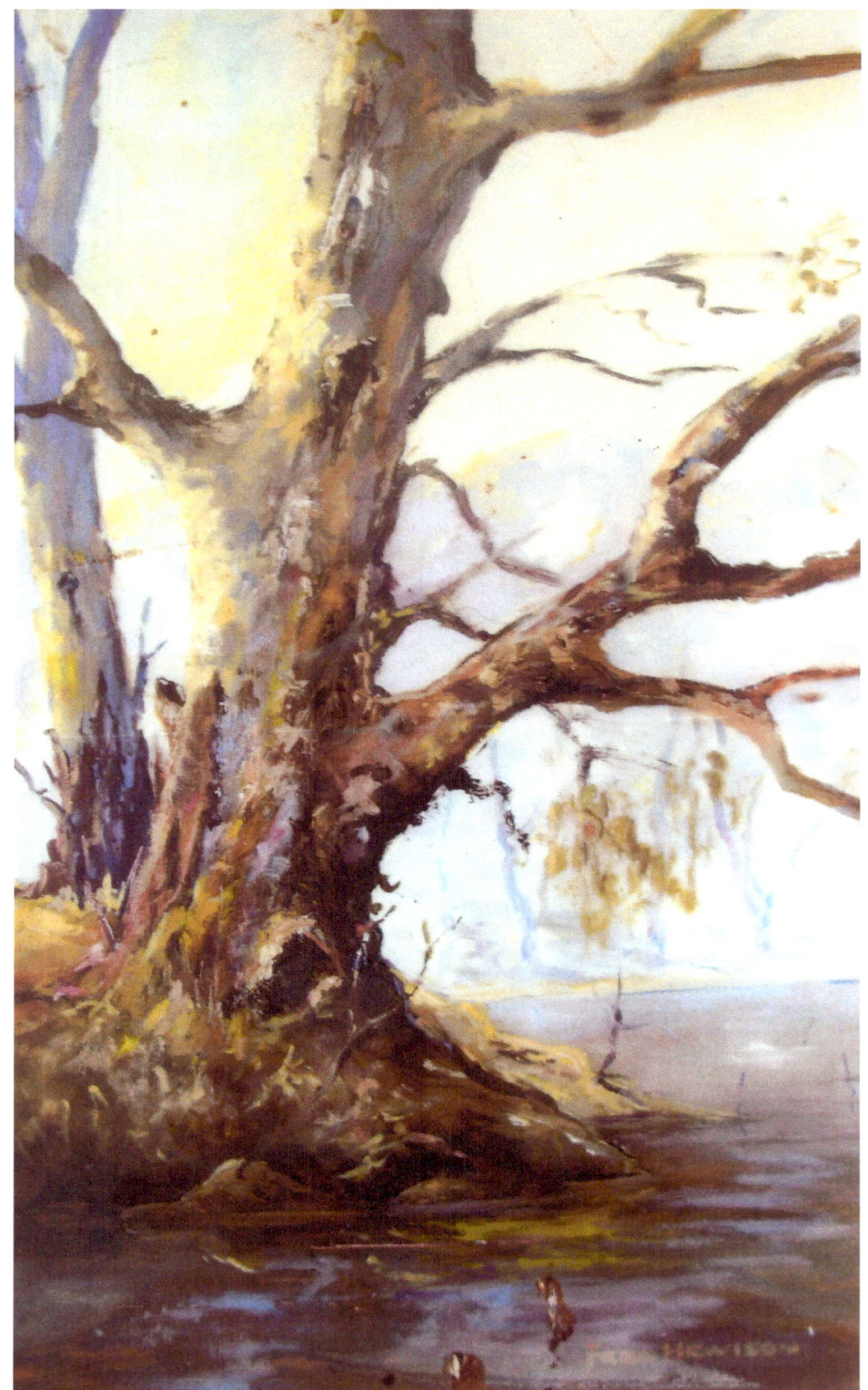

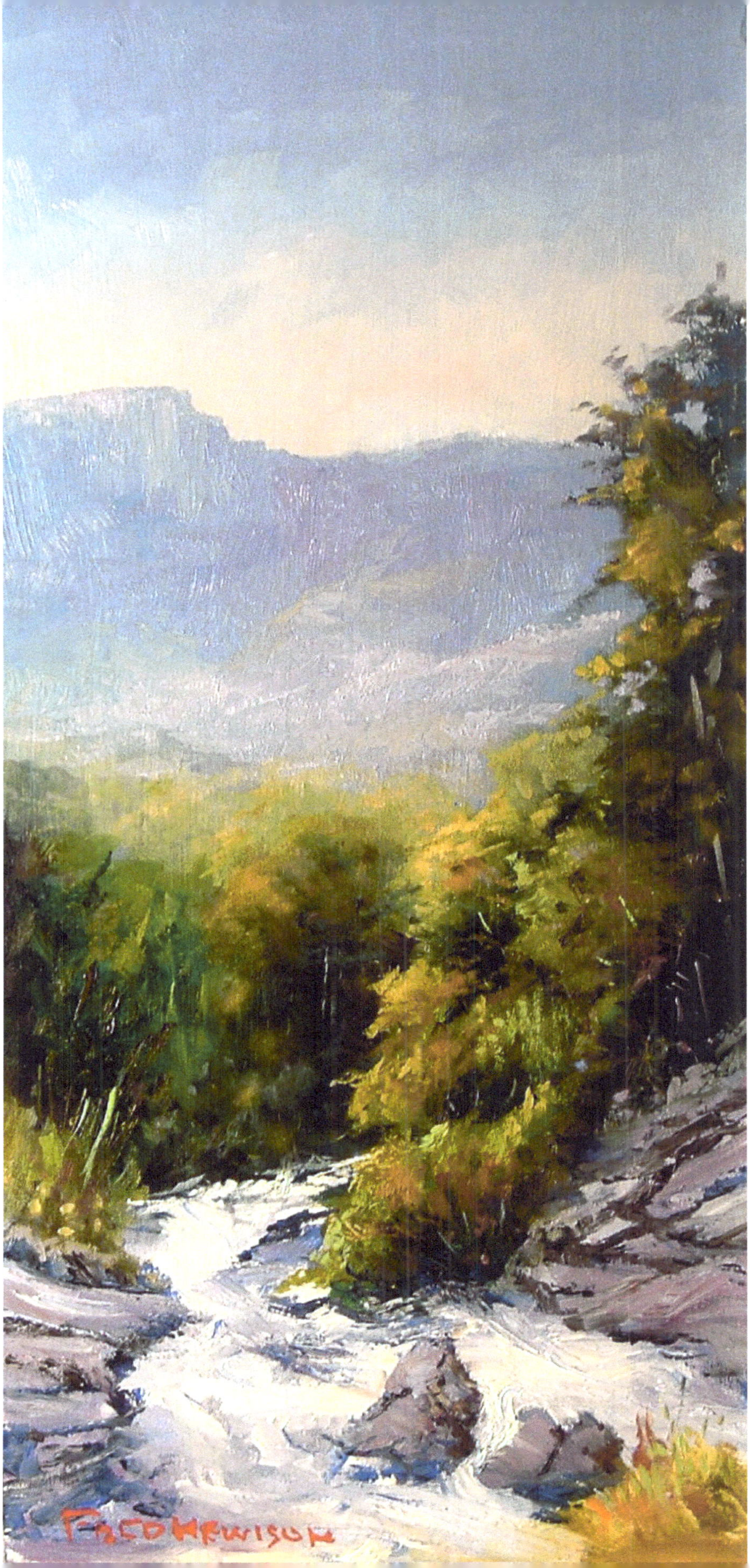

Ebor Falls, NSW

Clarence River, Grafton

Poplar, Clarence River

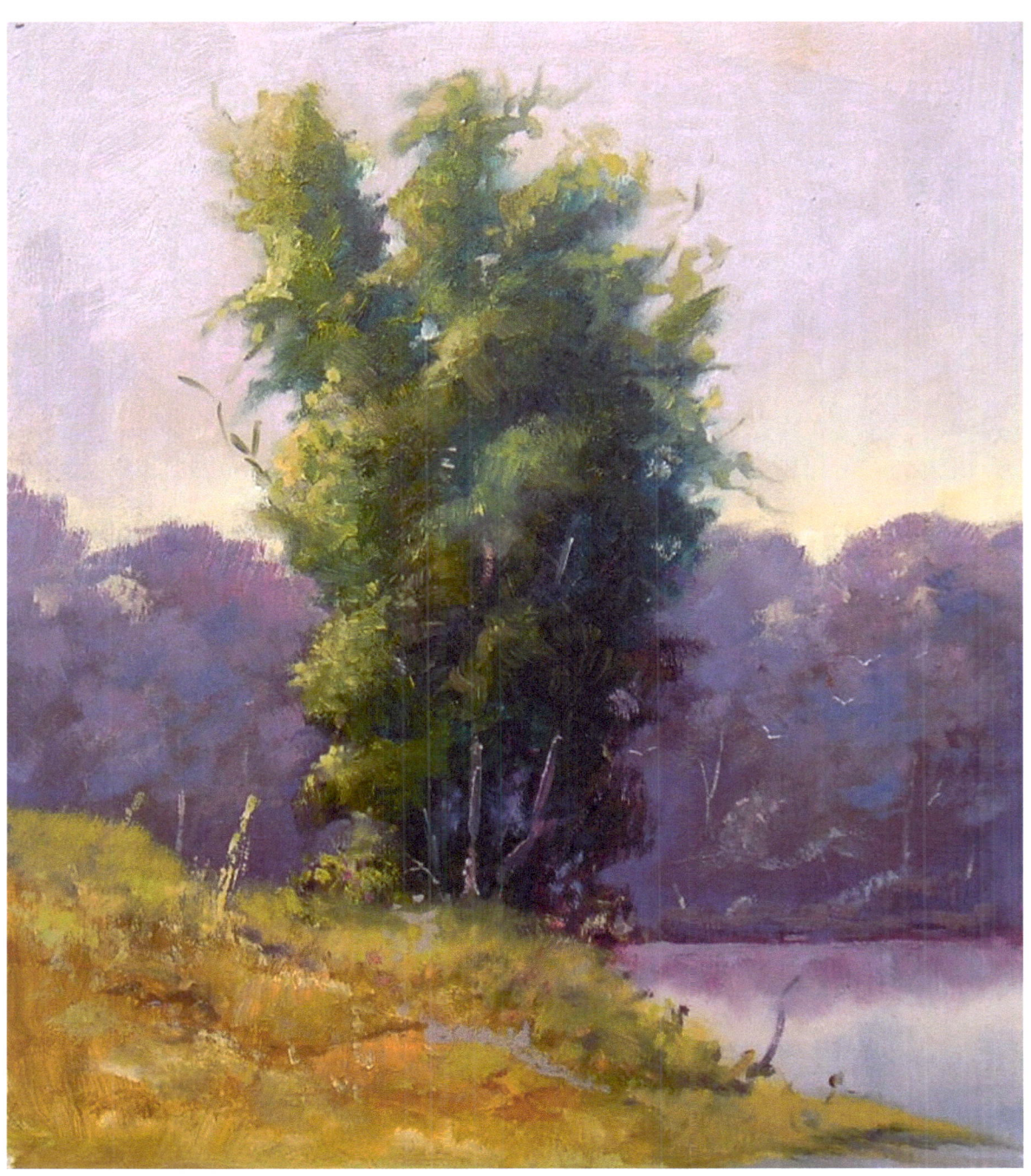

House on the Hill, Murwillumbah

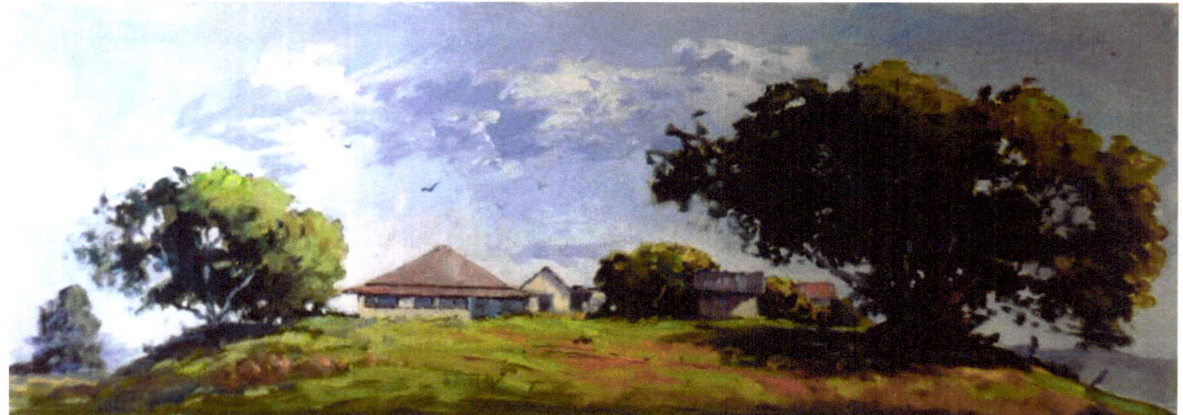

The Old Barn, Drake, NSW

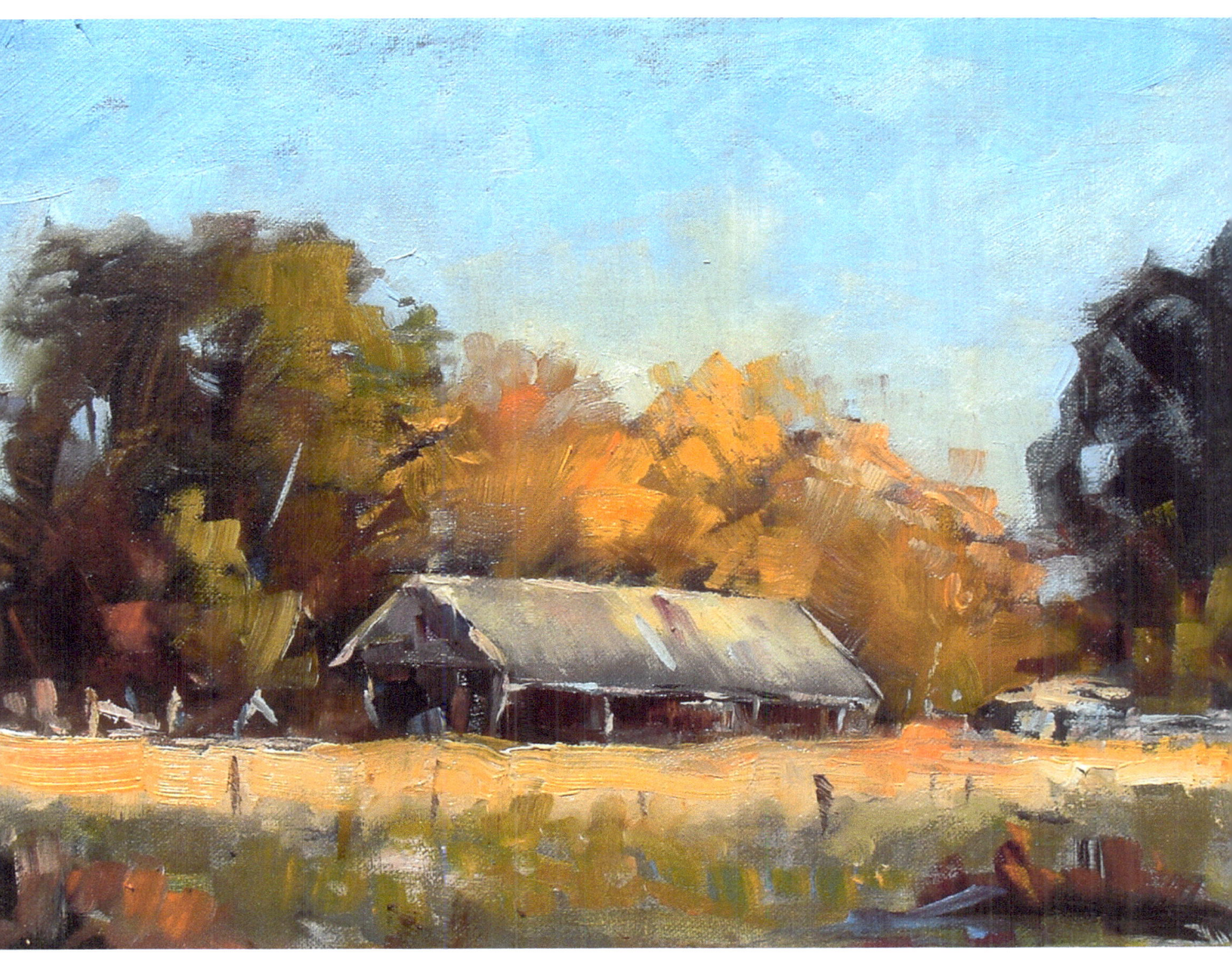

River Gums

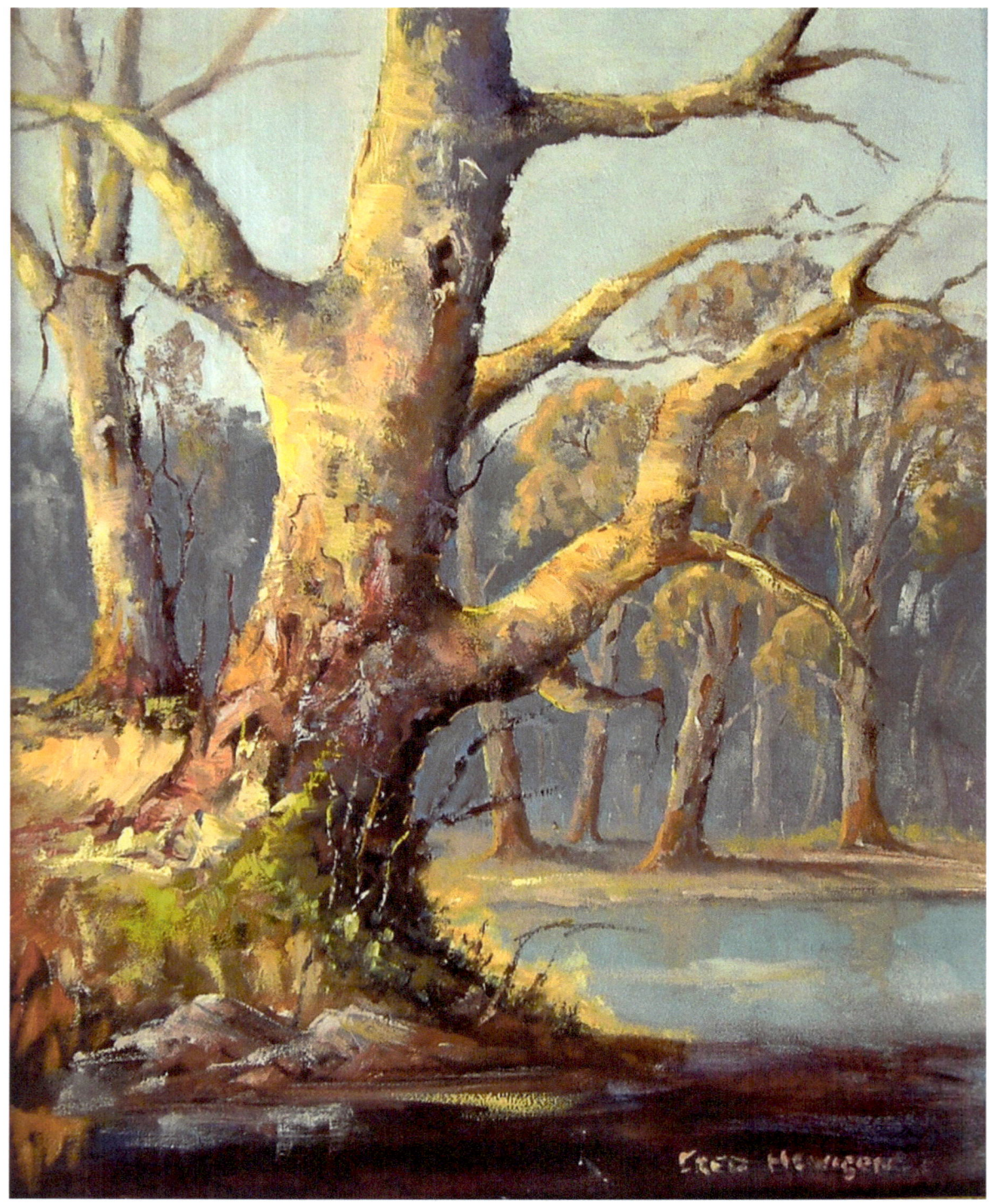

Clarence, Sunset

Rous River, NSW

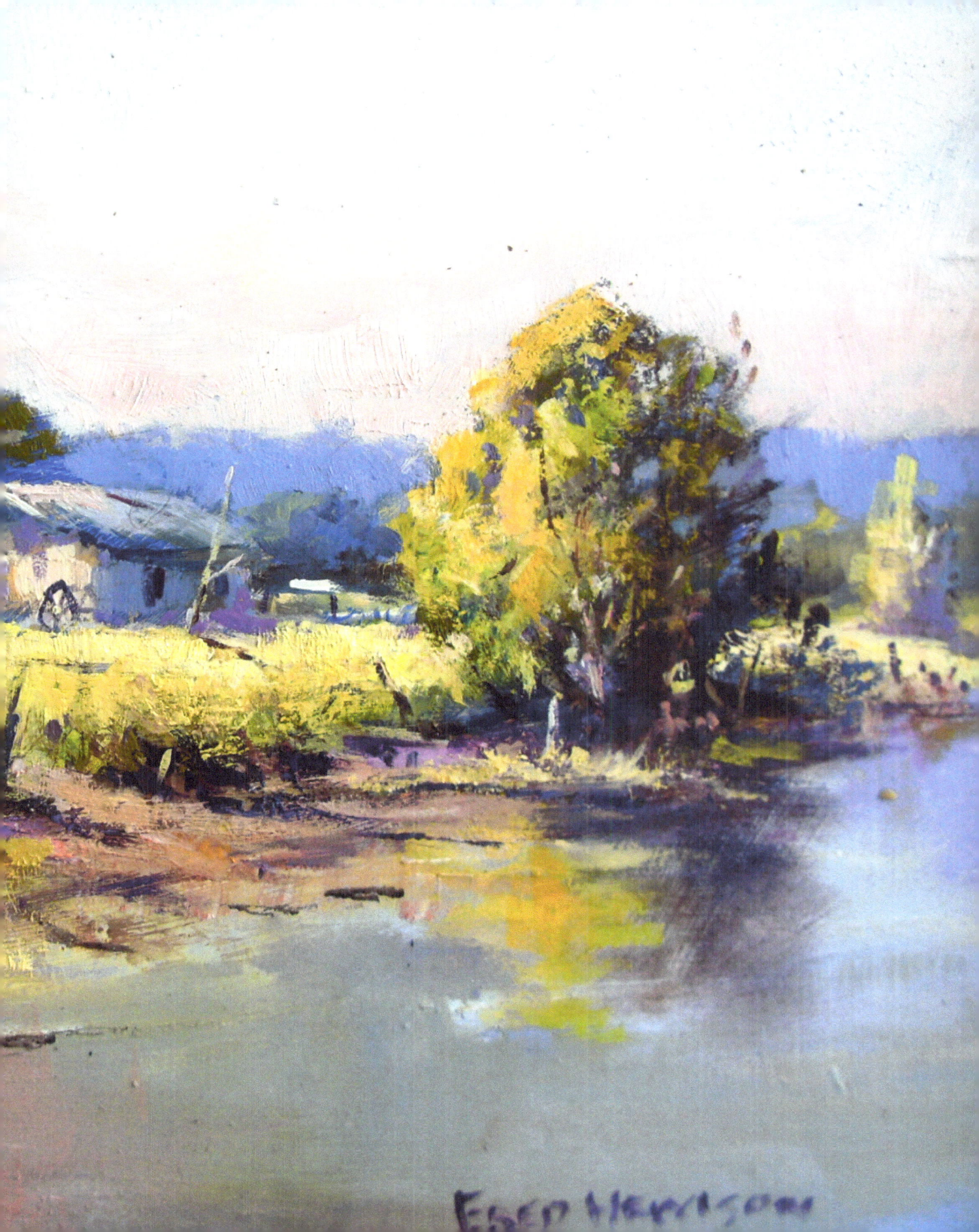

The Carence River, Grafton

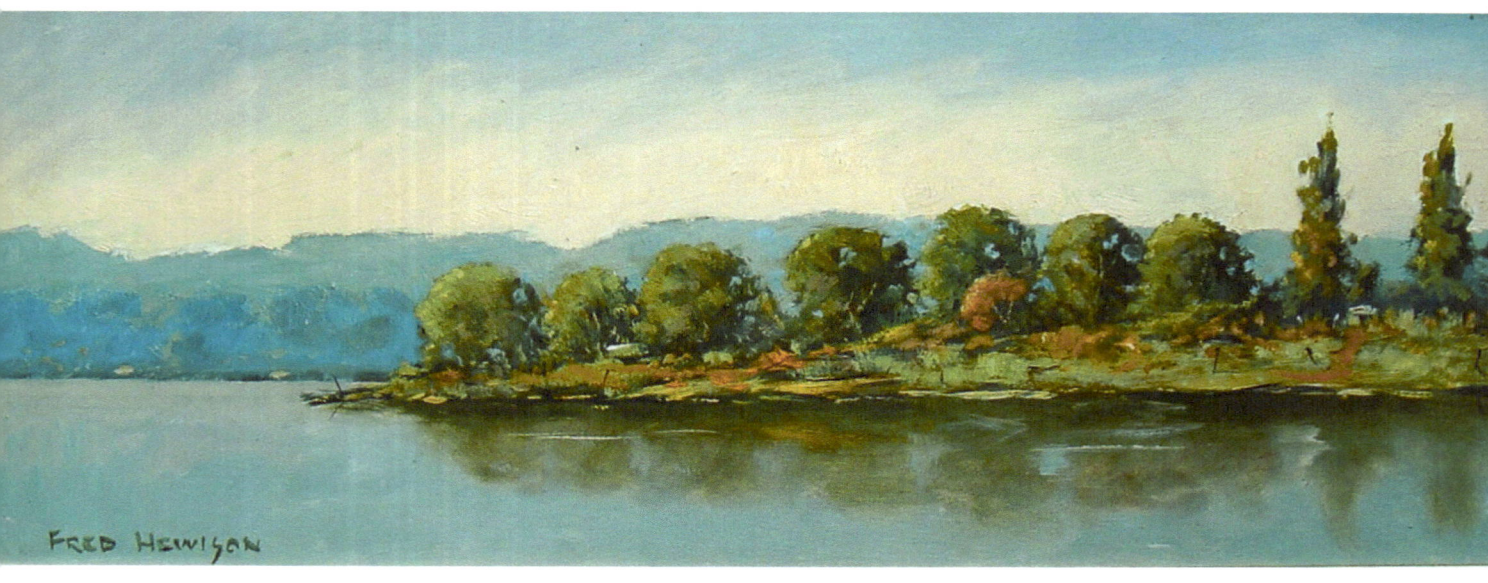

Copmanhurst, NSW

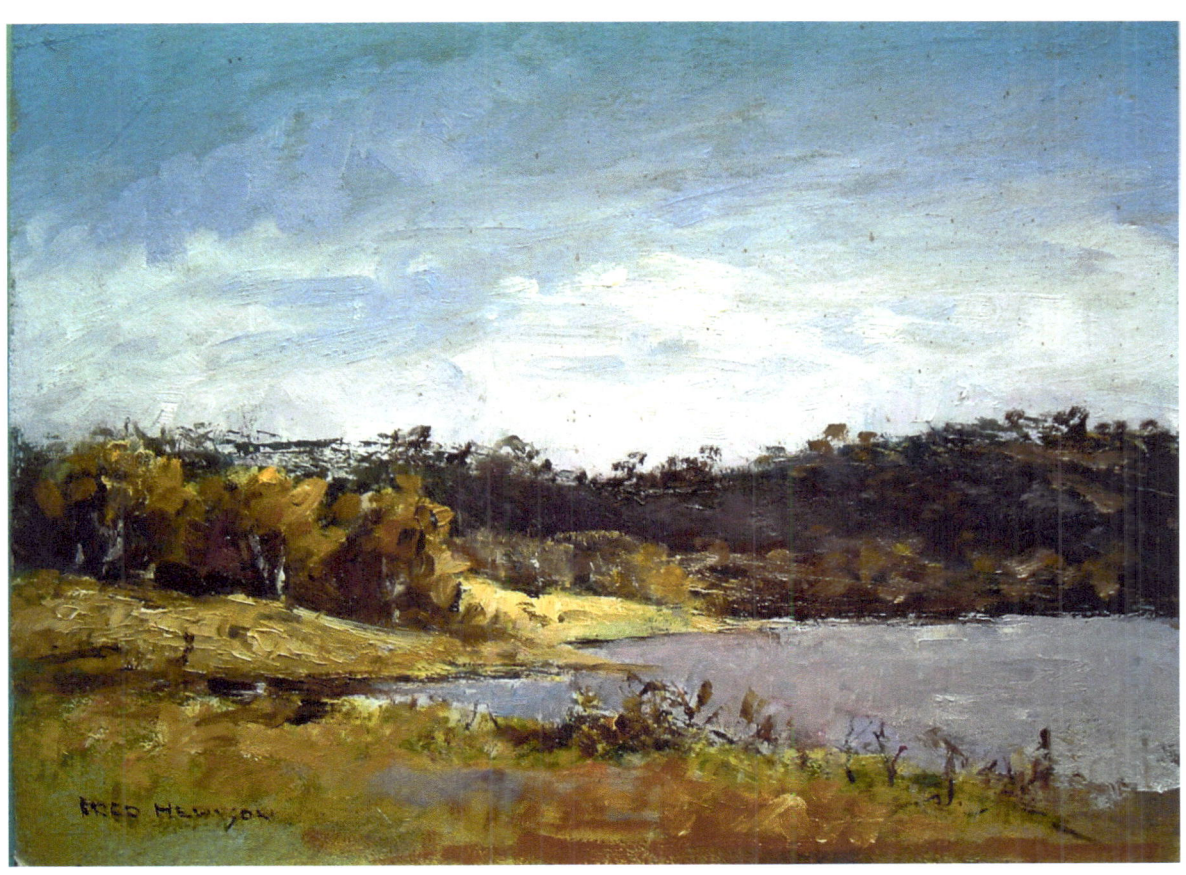

The Pond

Two Battlers

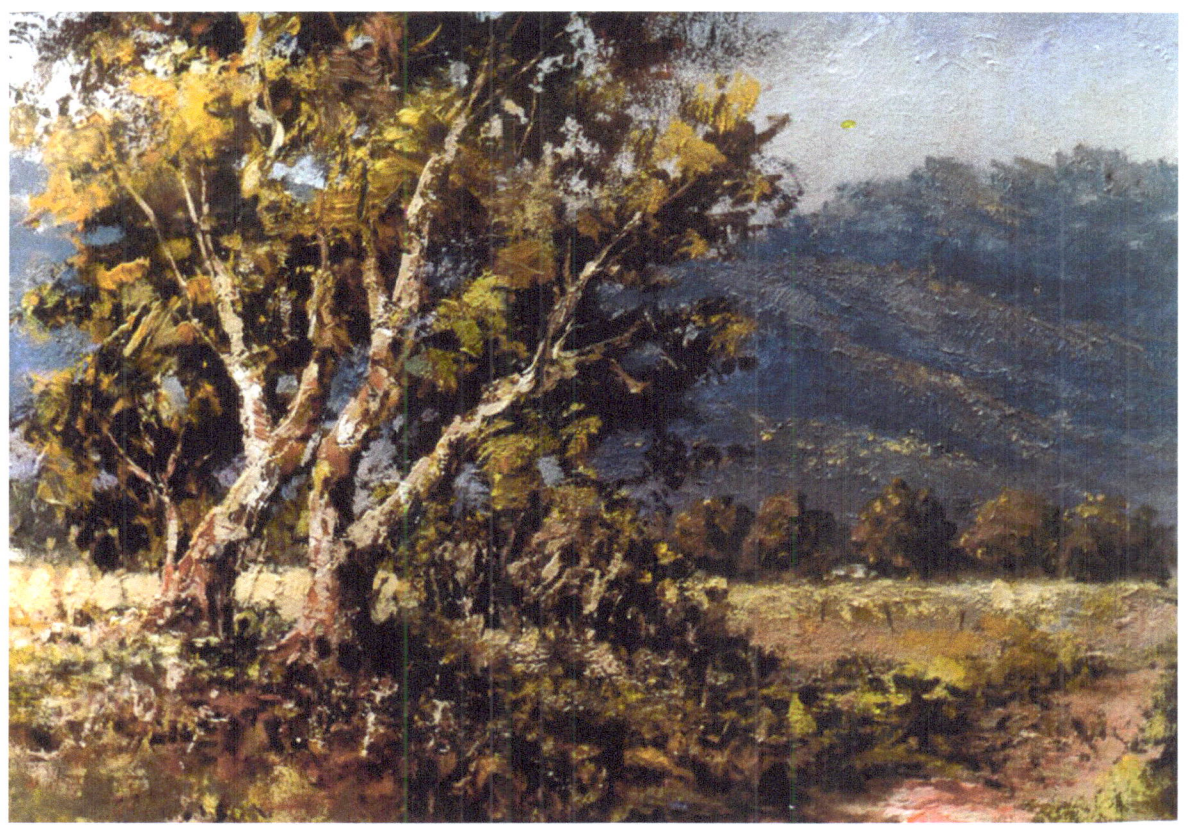

Copacabana to Terrigal, NSW

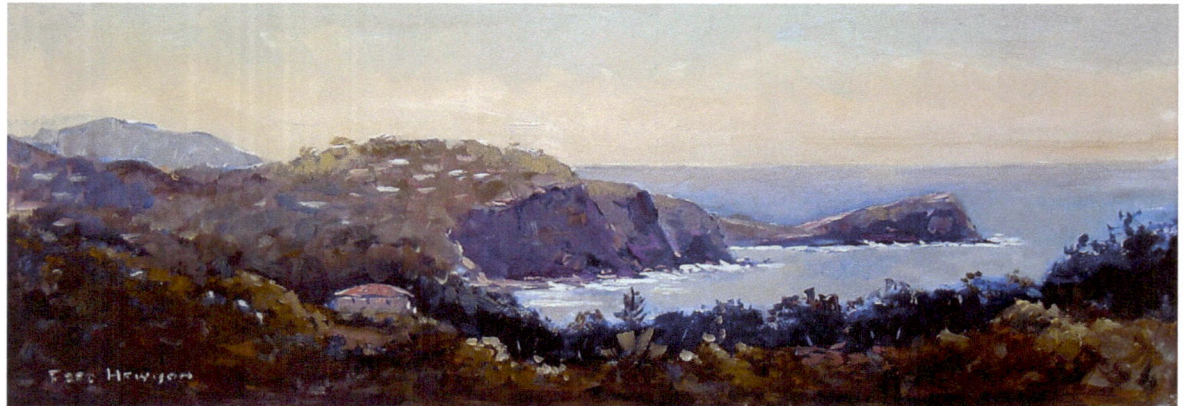

The Tweed River

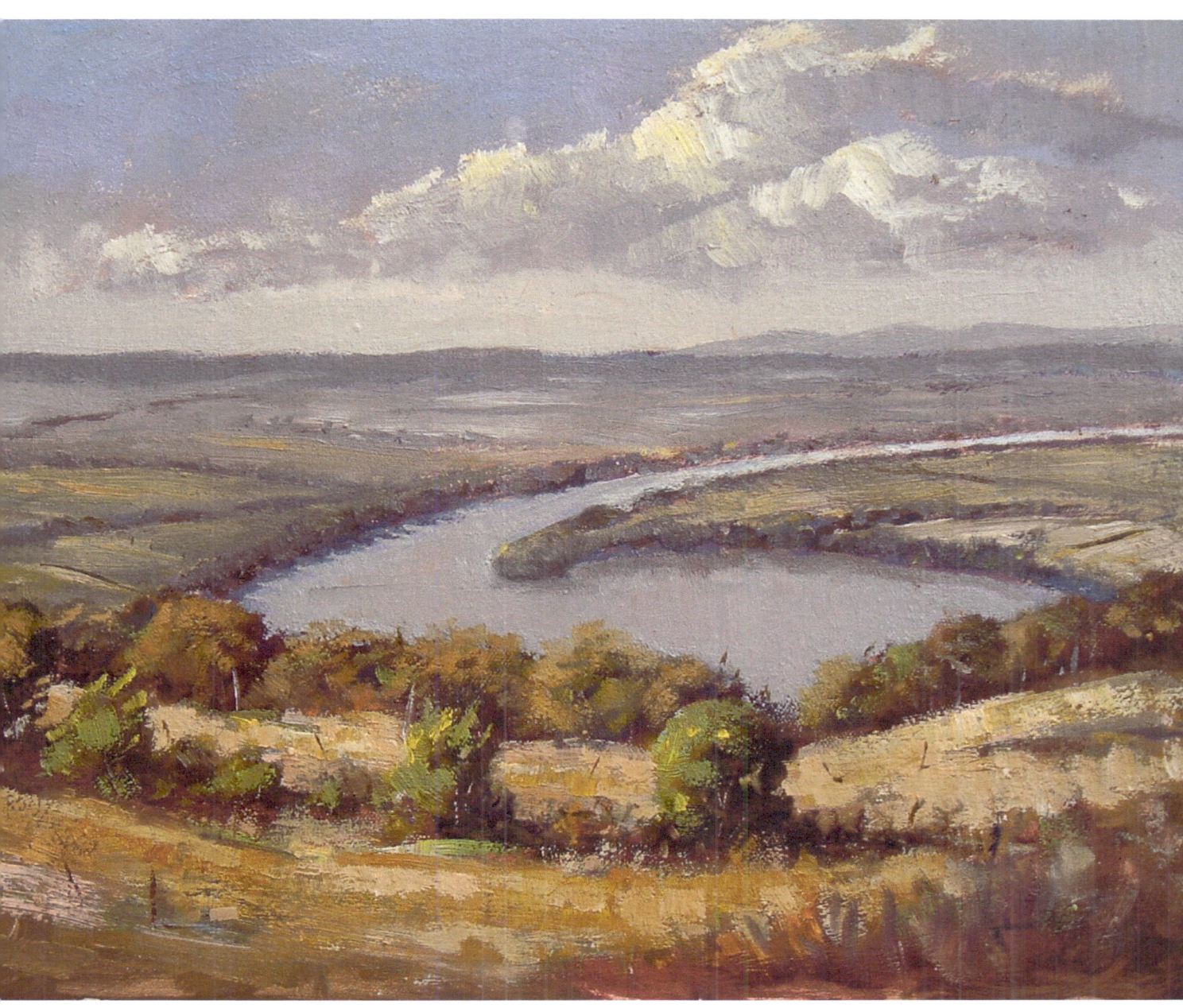

Tweed River

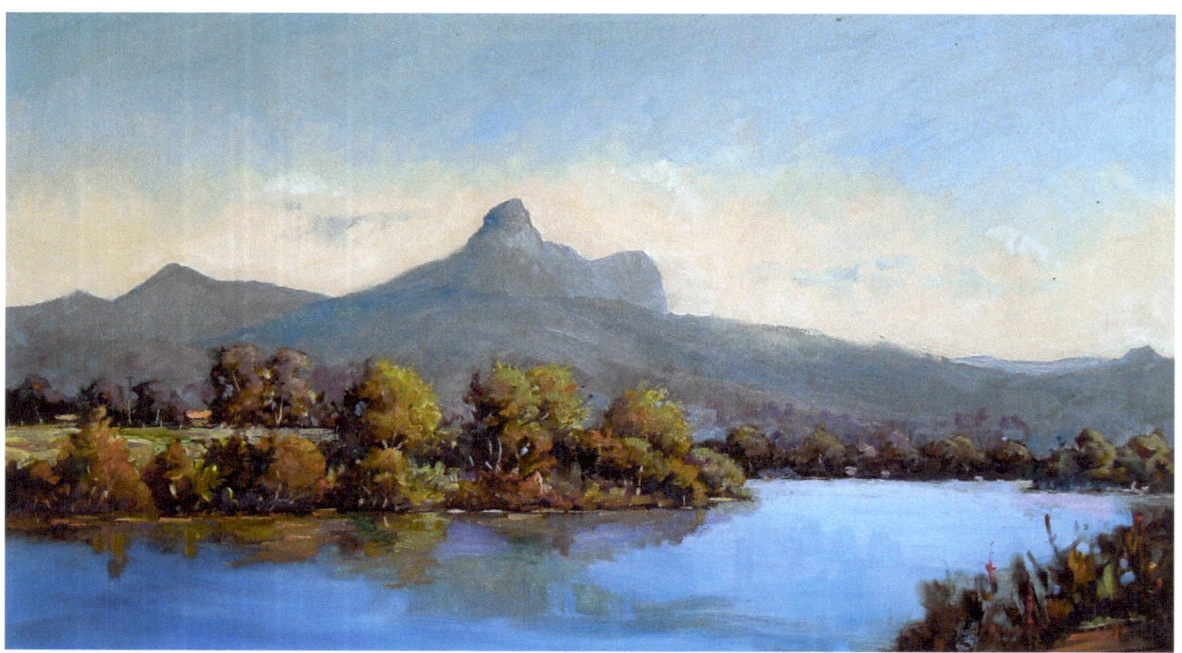

Tweed Valley

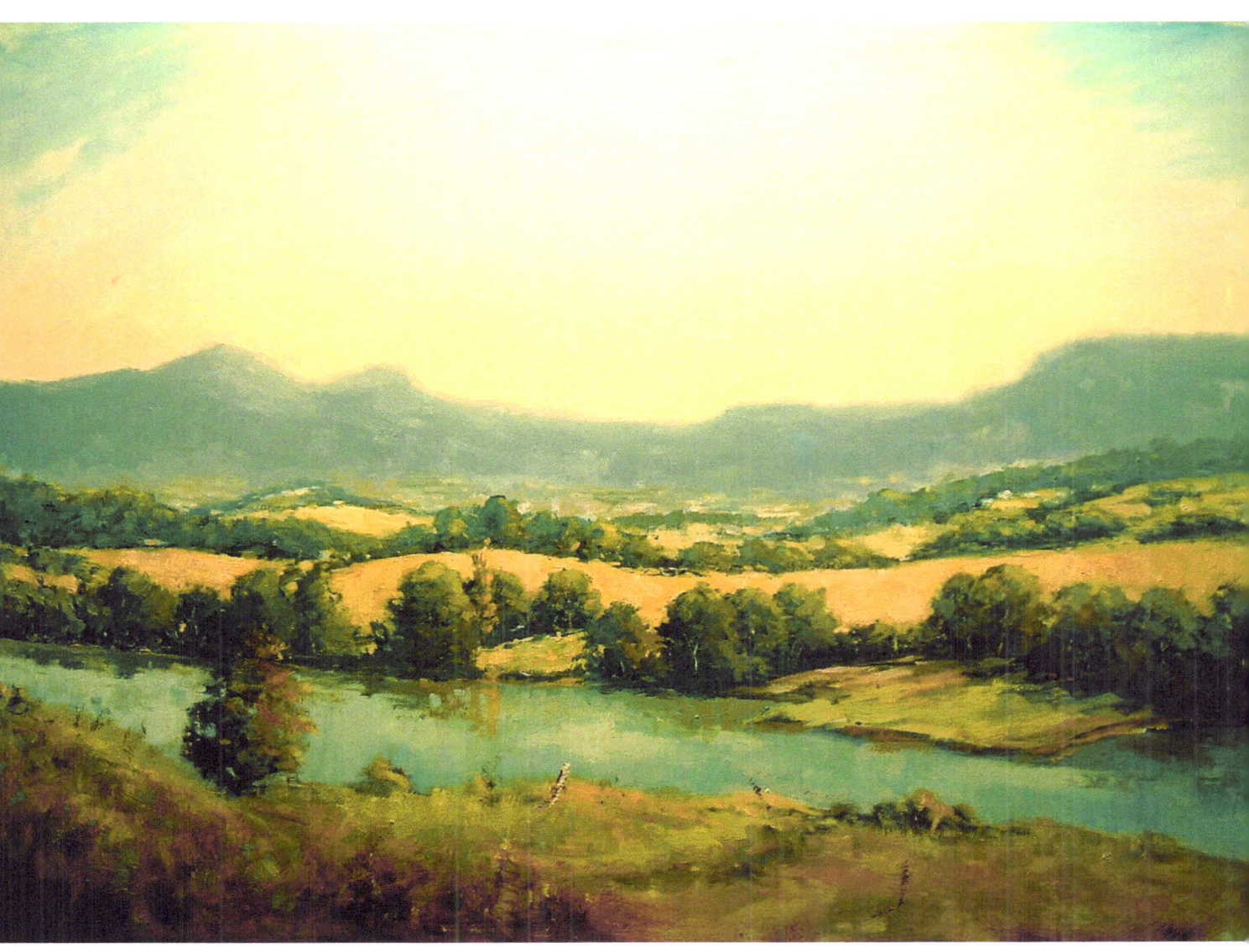

Emmaville, NSW

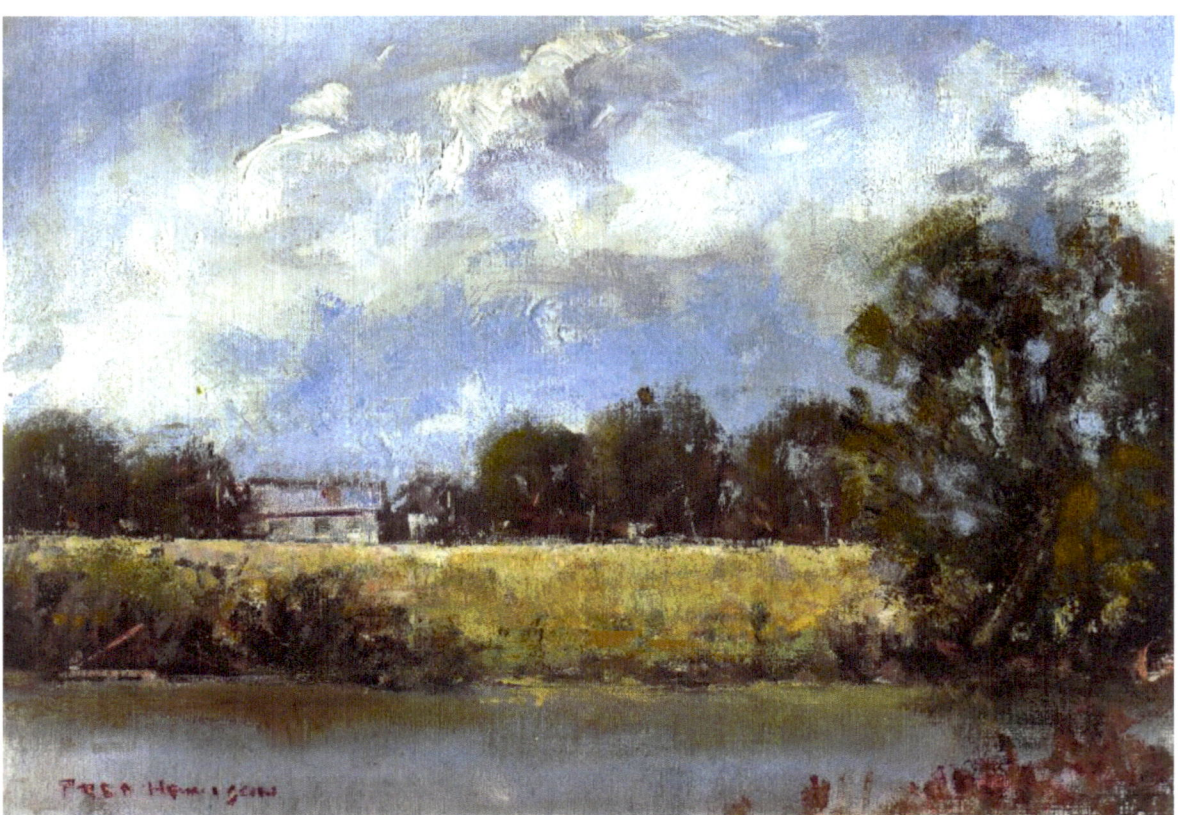

A Hot Day

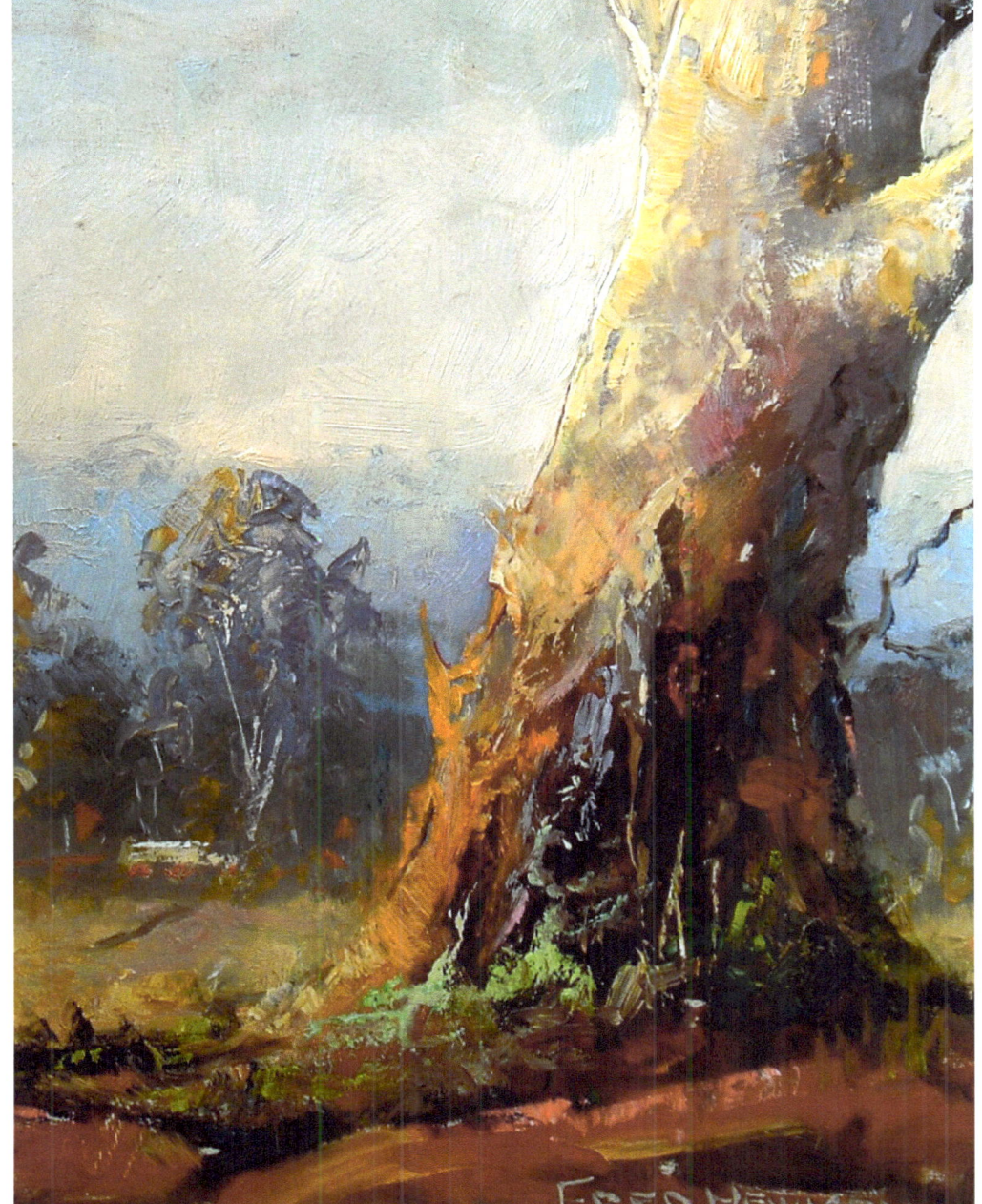

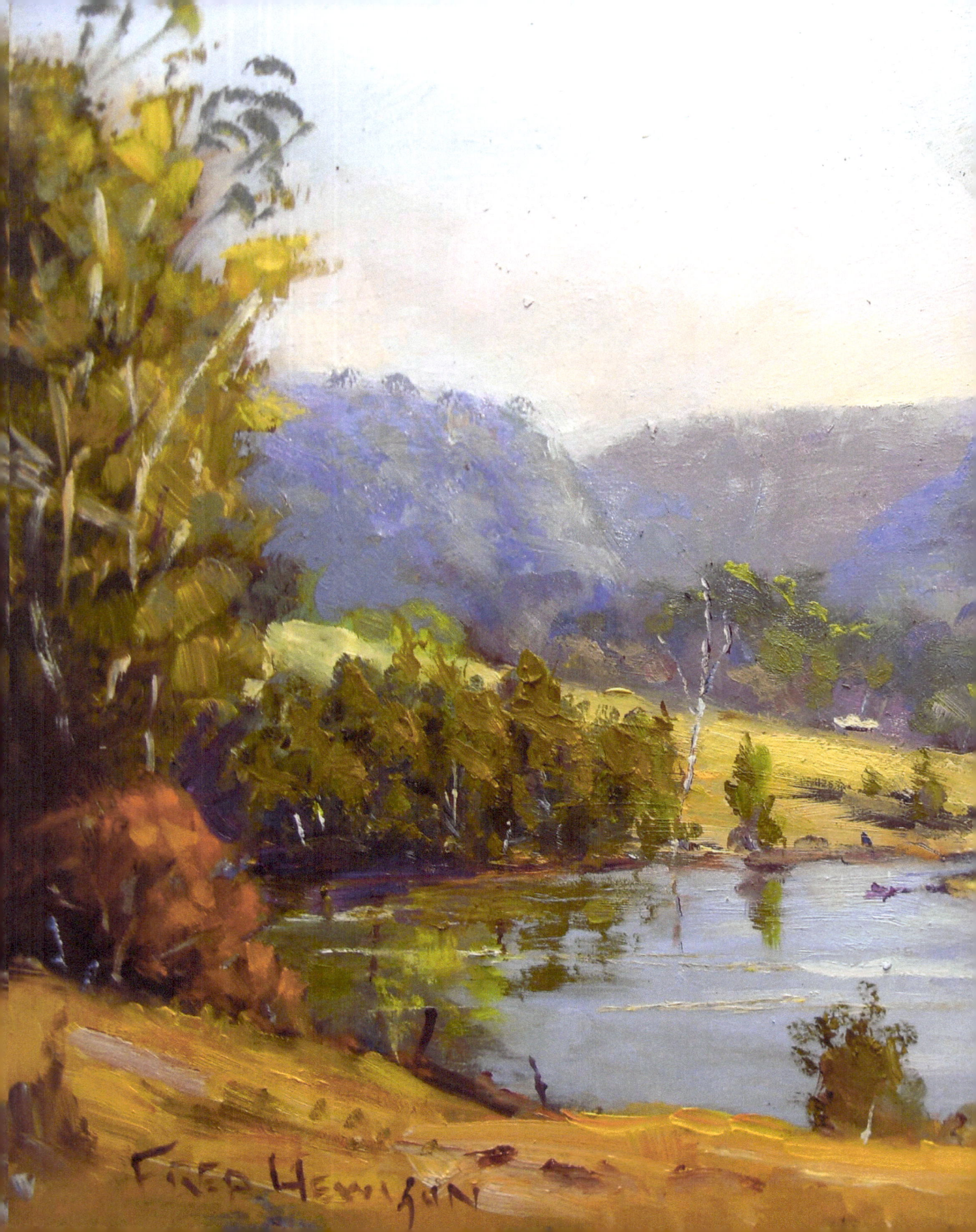

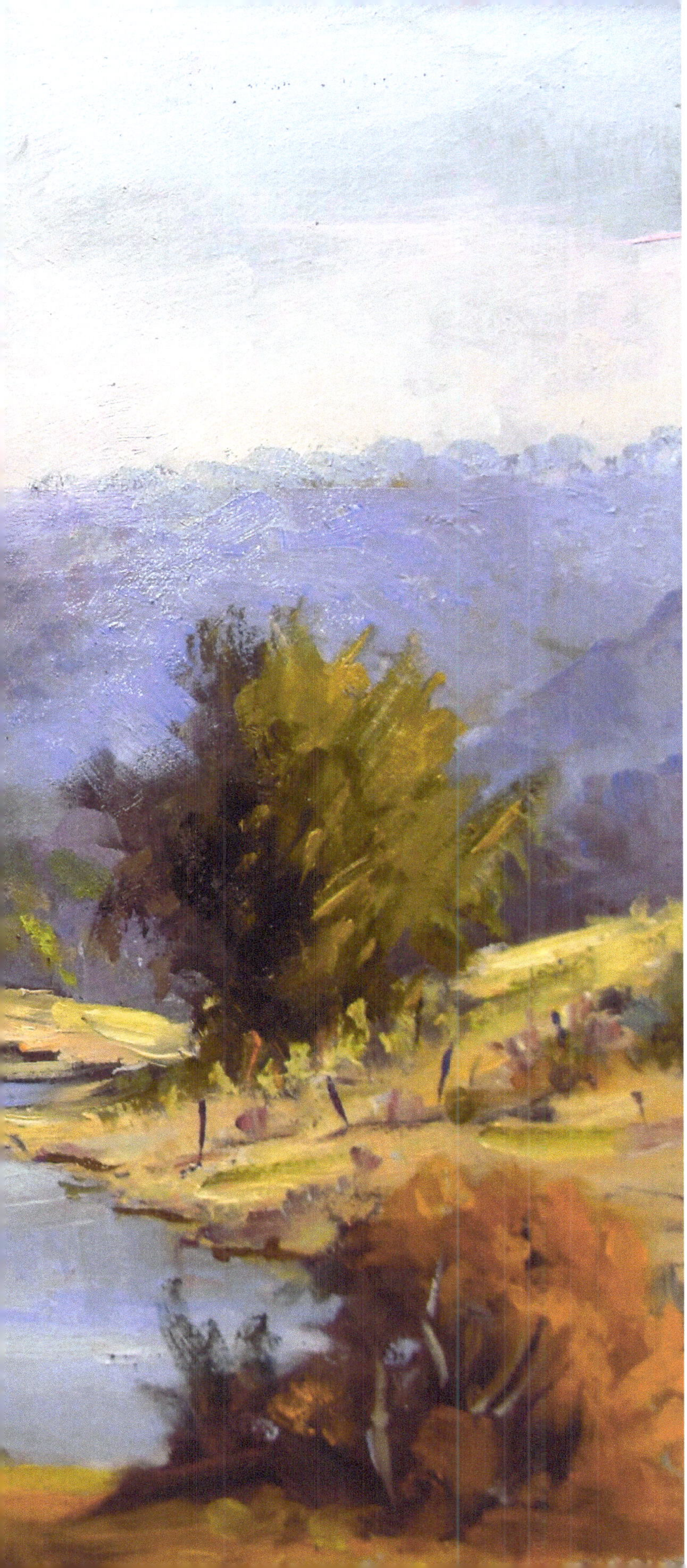

Upper Wilson (2)

Old Gum

FRED HEWISON

Tweed from Regional Gallery

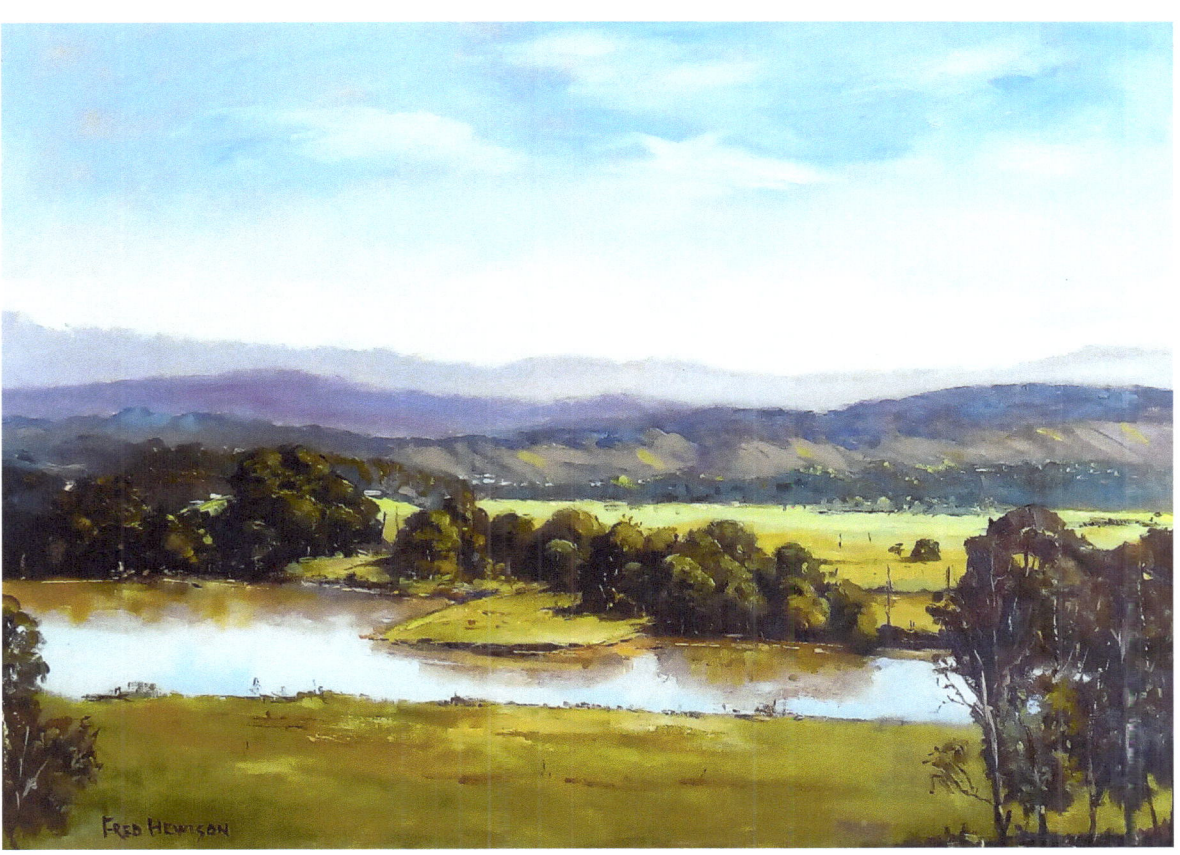

Tweed River

Long Gone

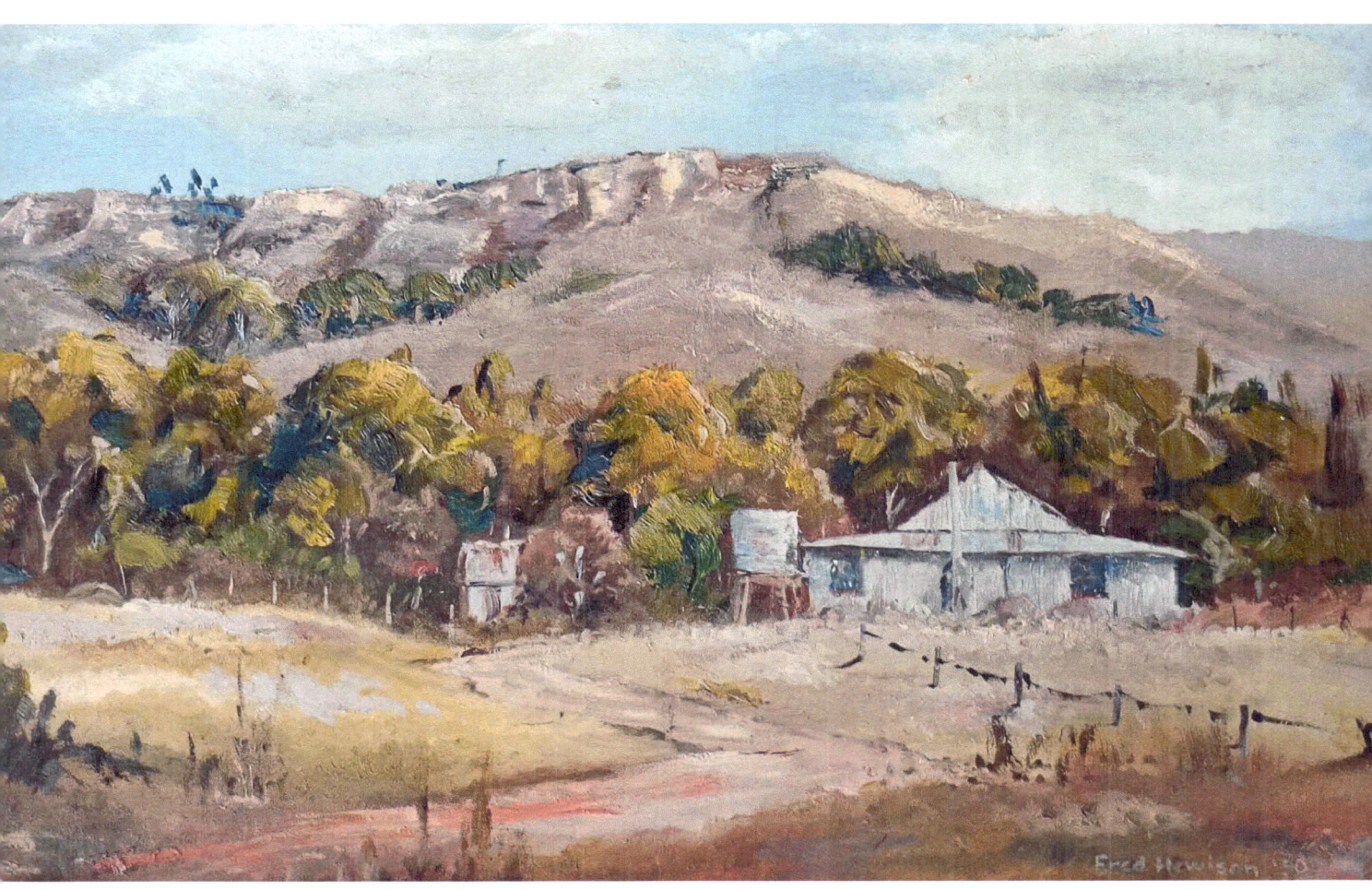

From Terranora, NSW

Kangaroo Creek, NSW

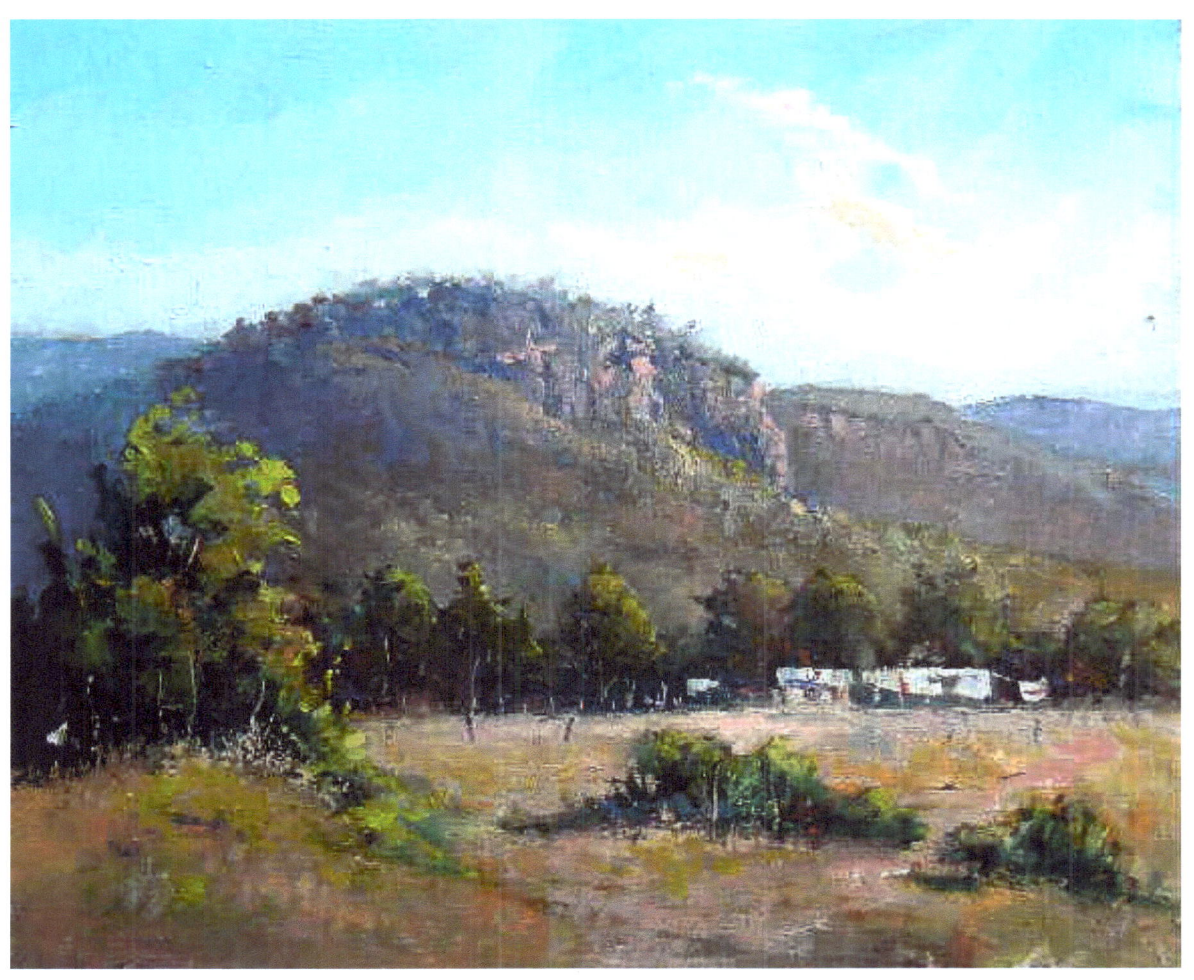

The Other Side

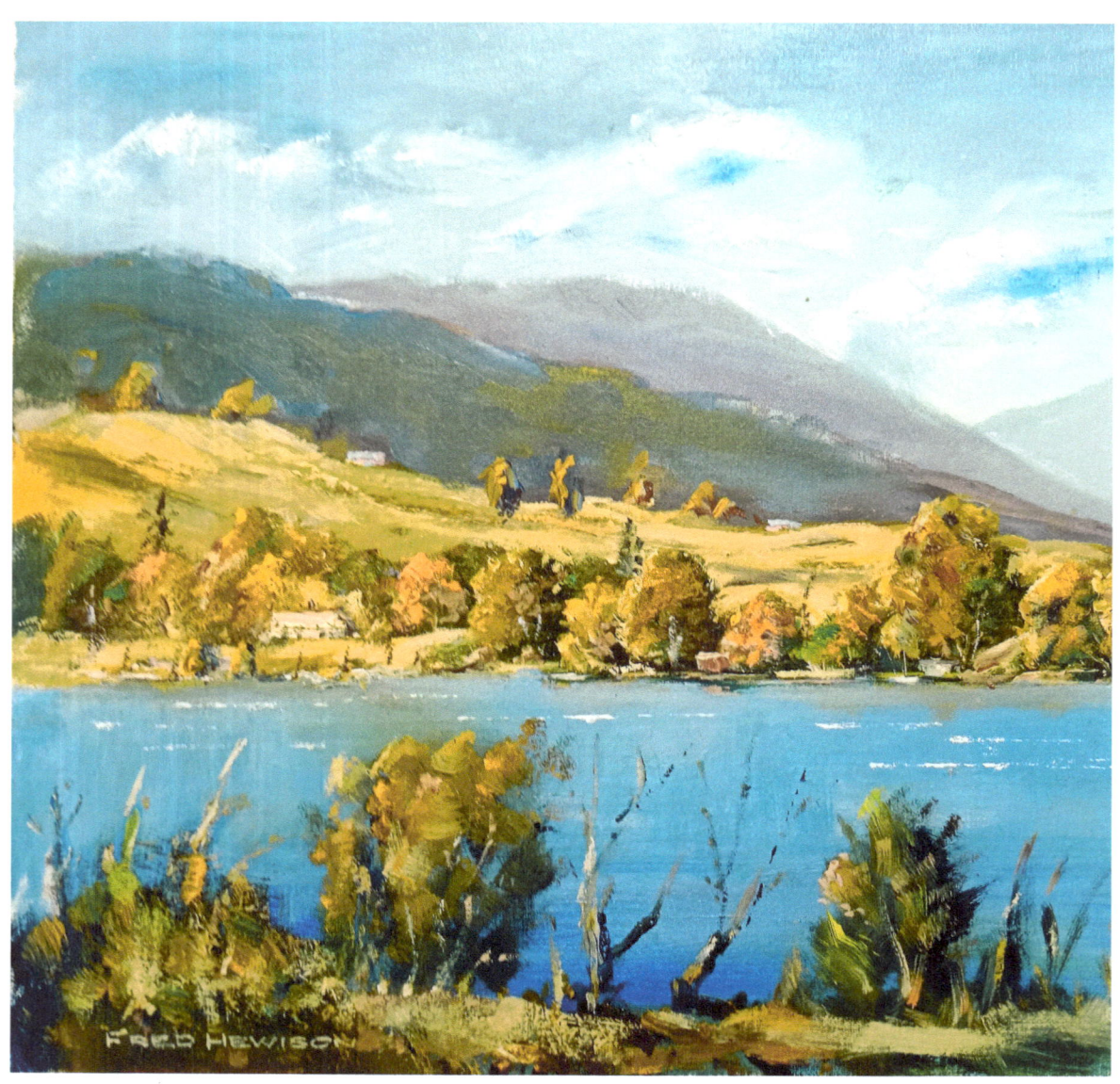

Of Past Times

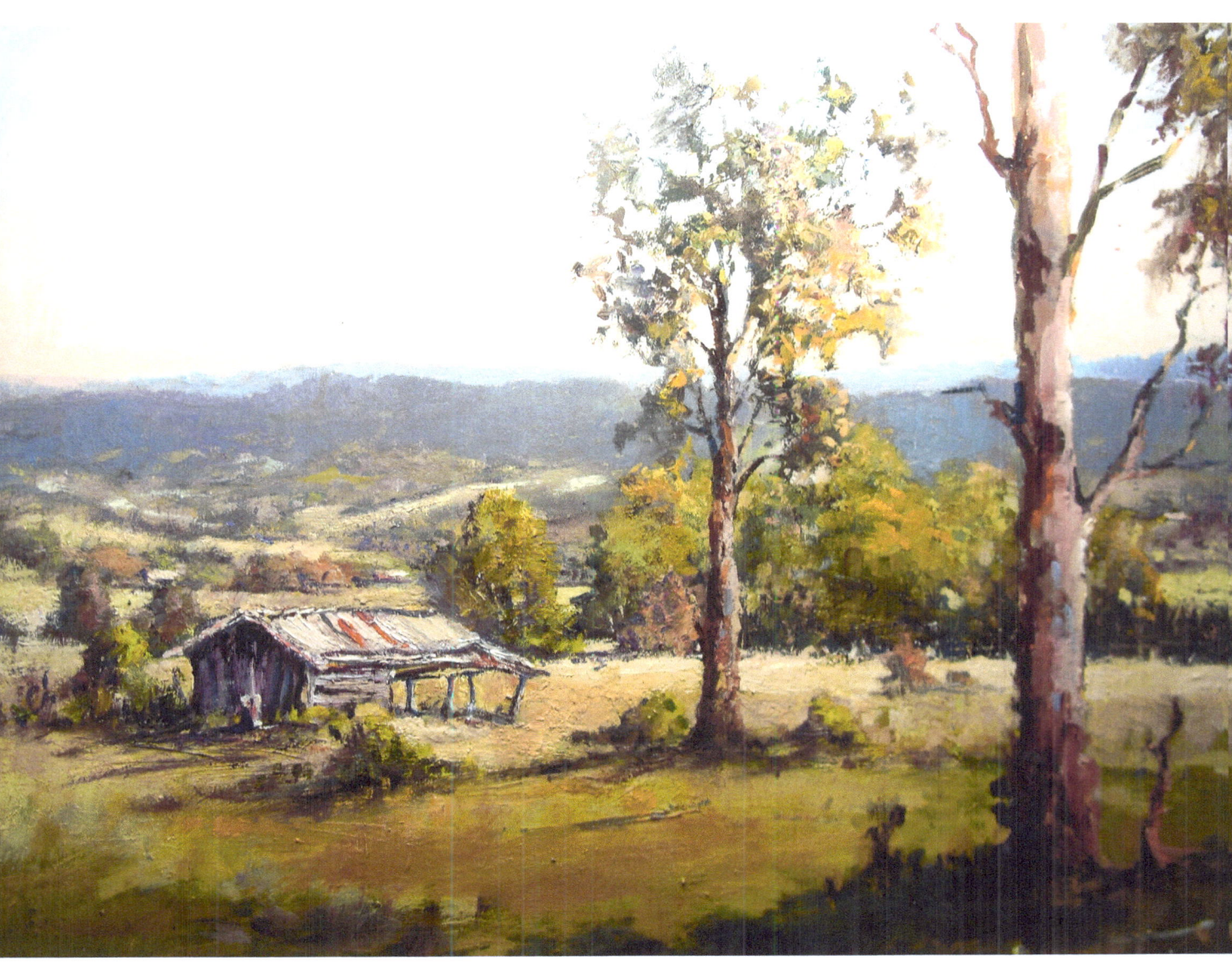

Autumn

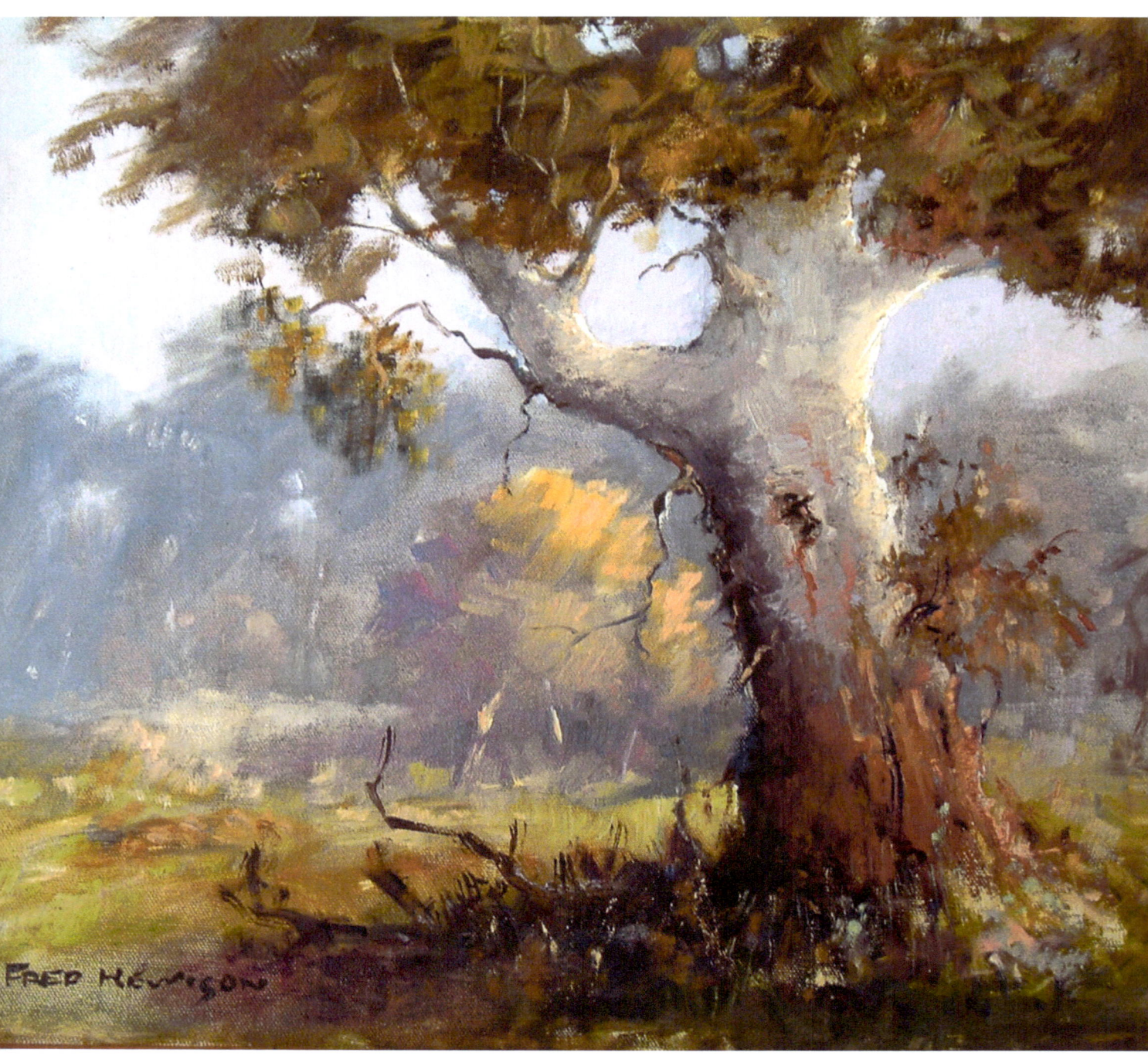

King George Falls, WA

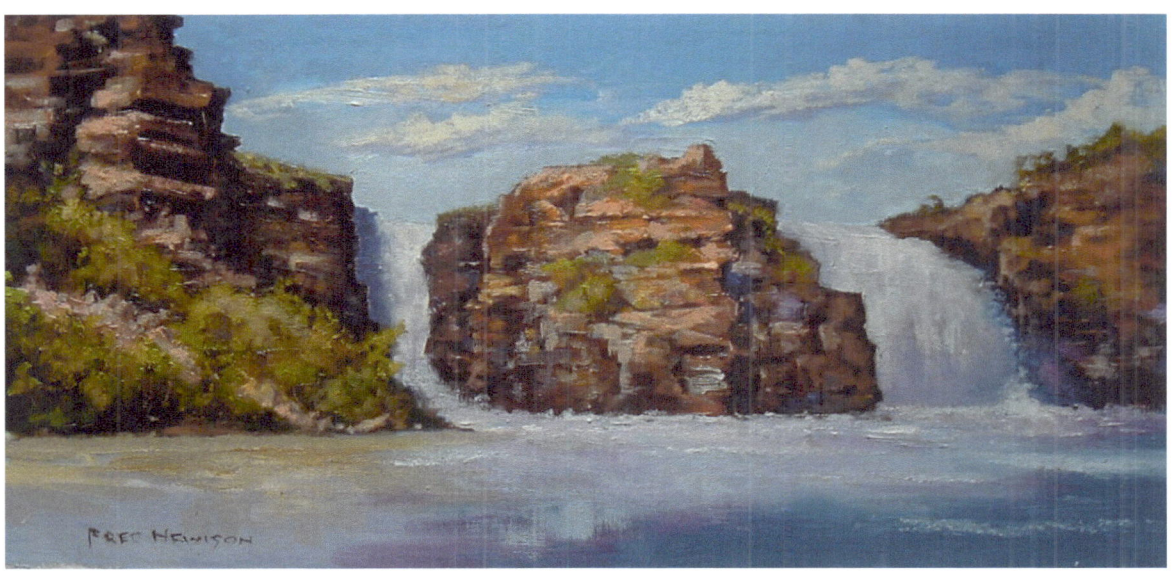

Early Morn, Bilambil Heights

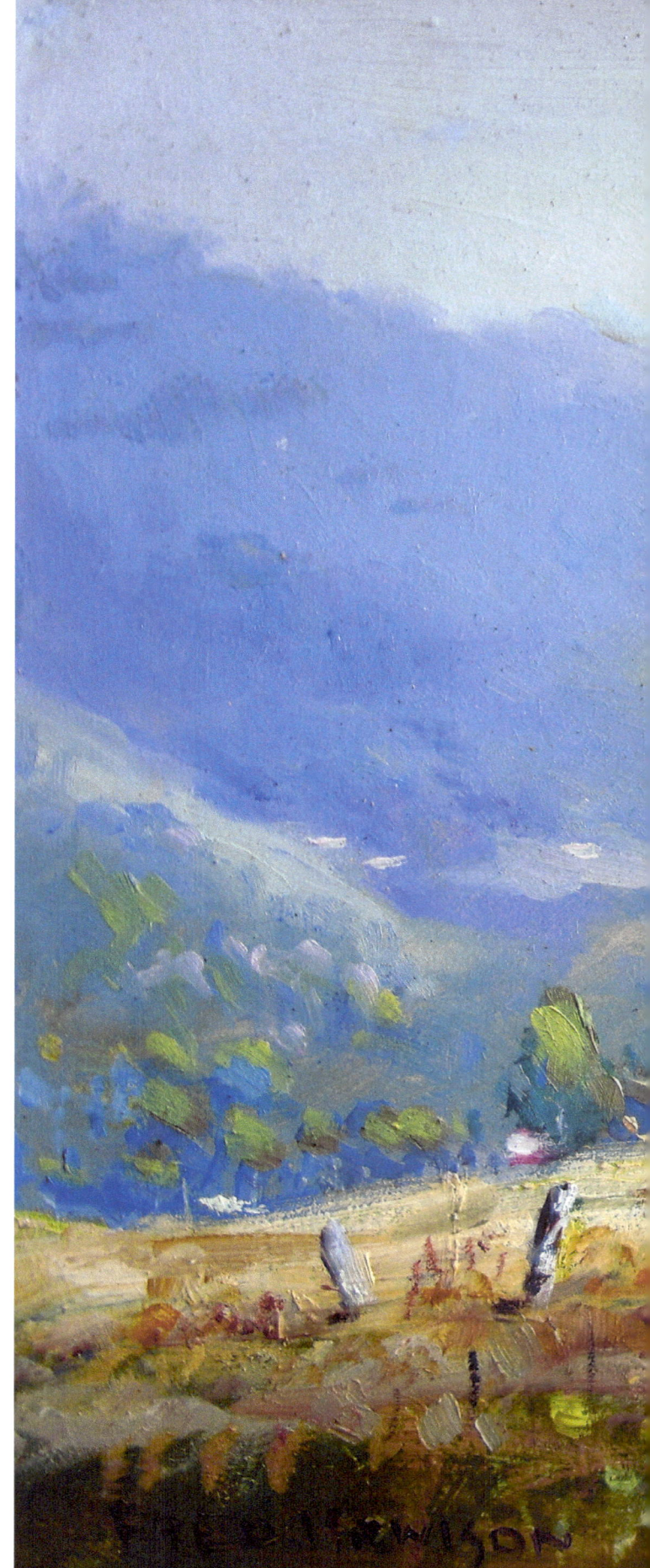

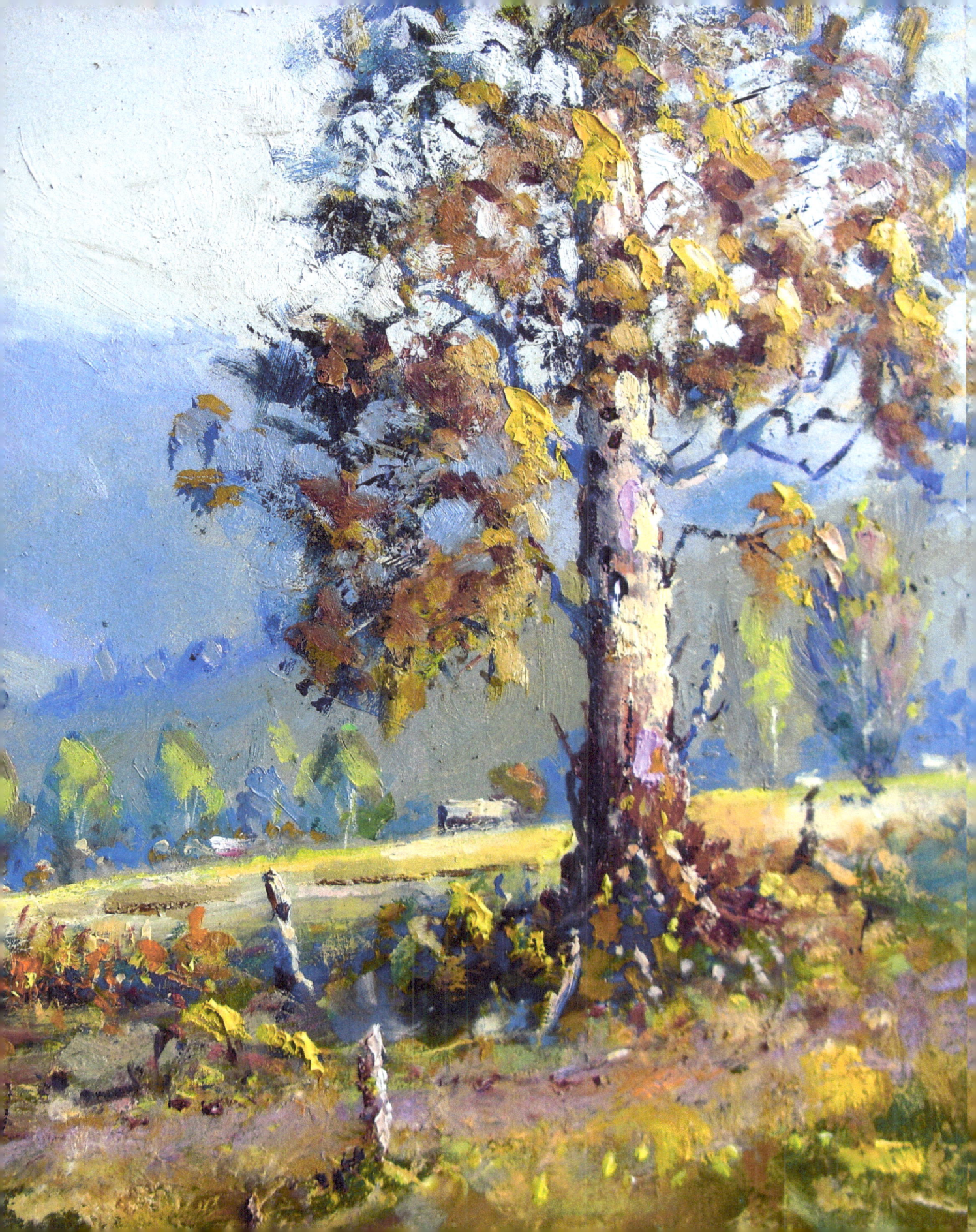

Mount Egmont, NZ

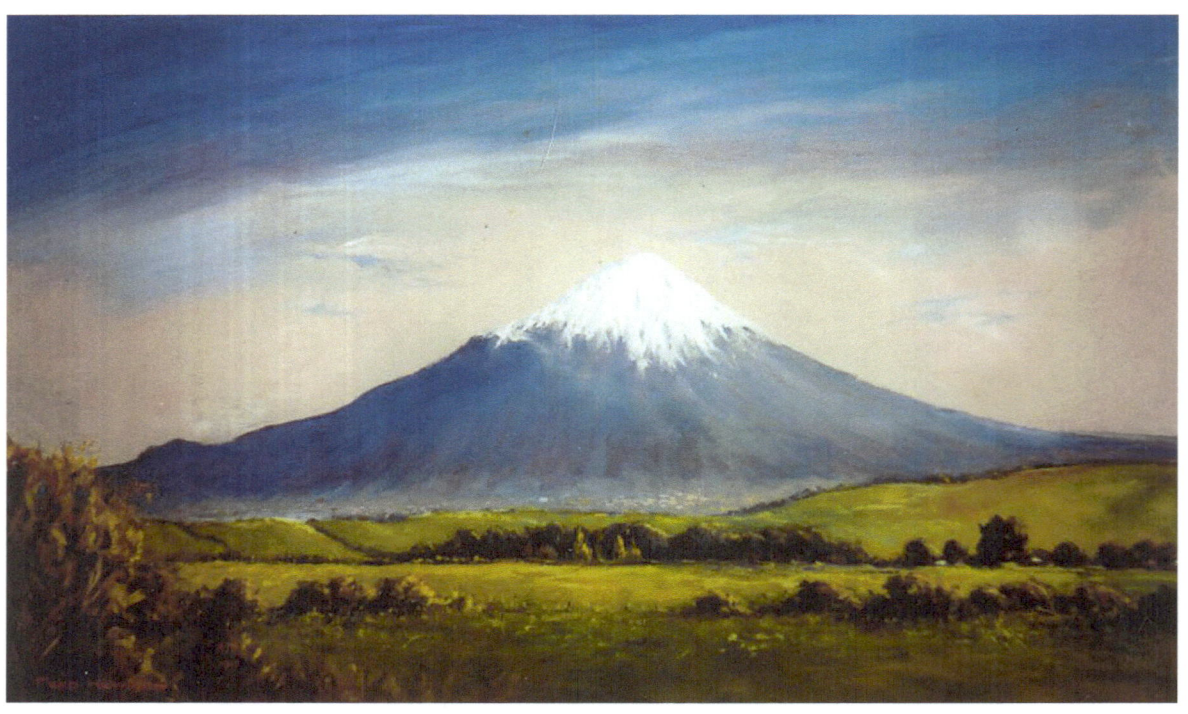

Mount Warning from Tweed

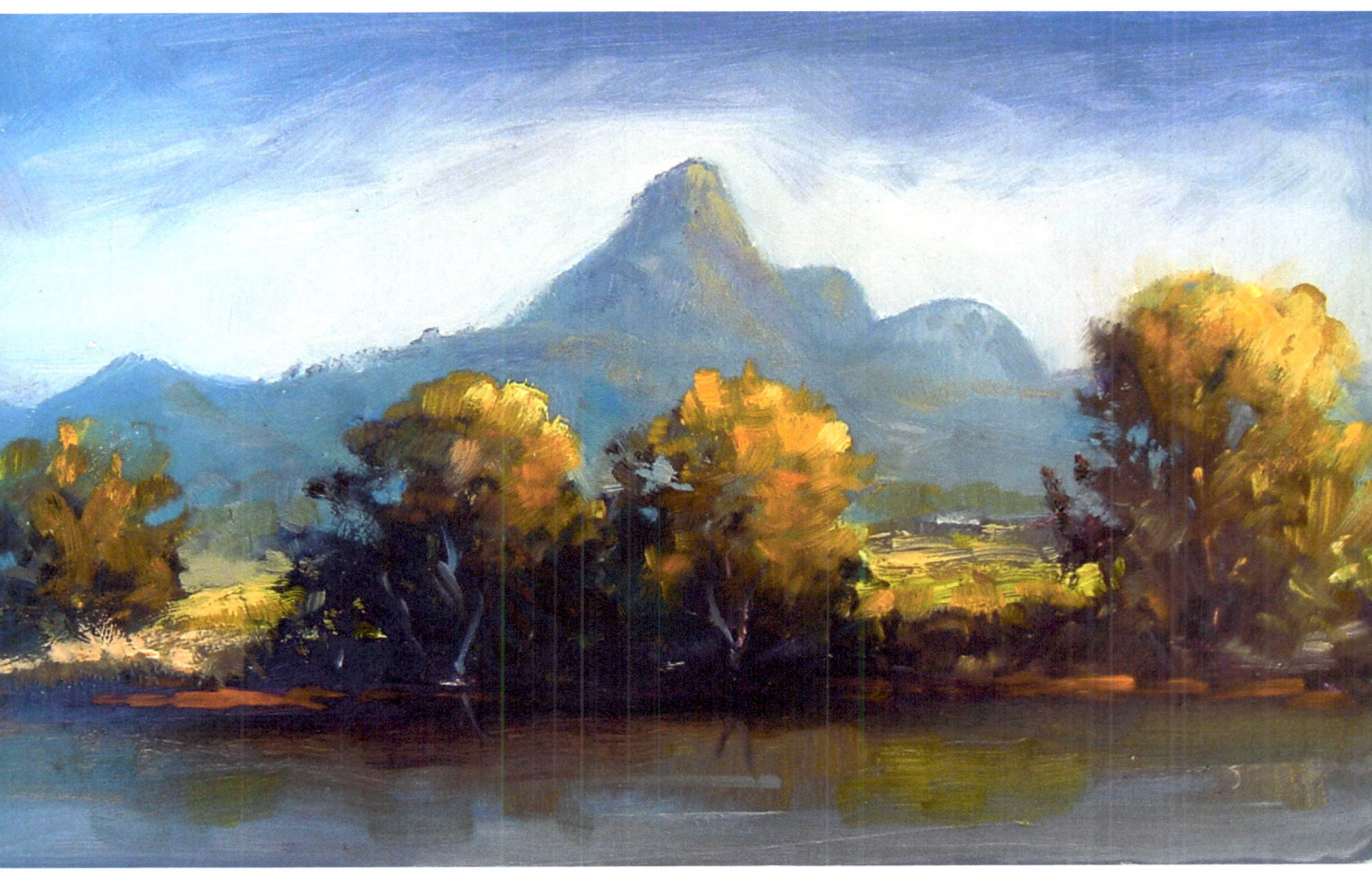

Quick Sketch in Oils

Upper Wilson River

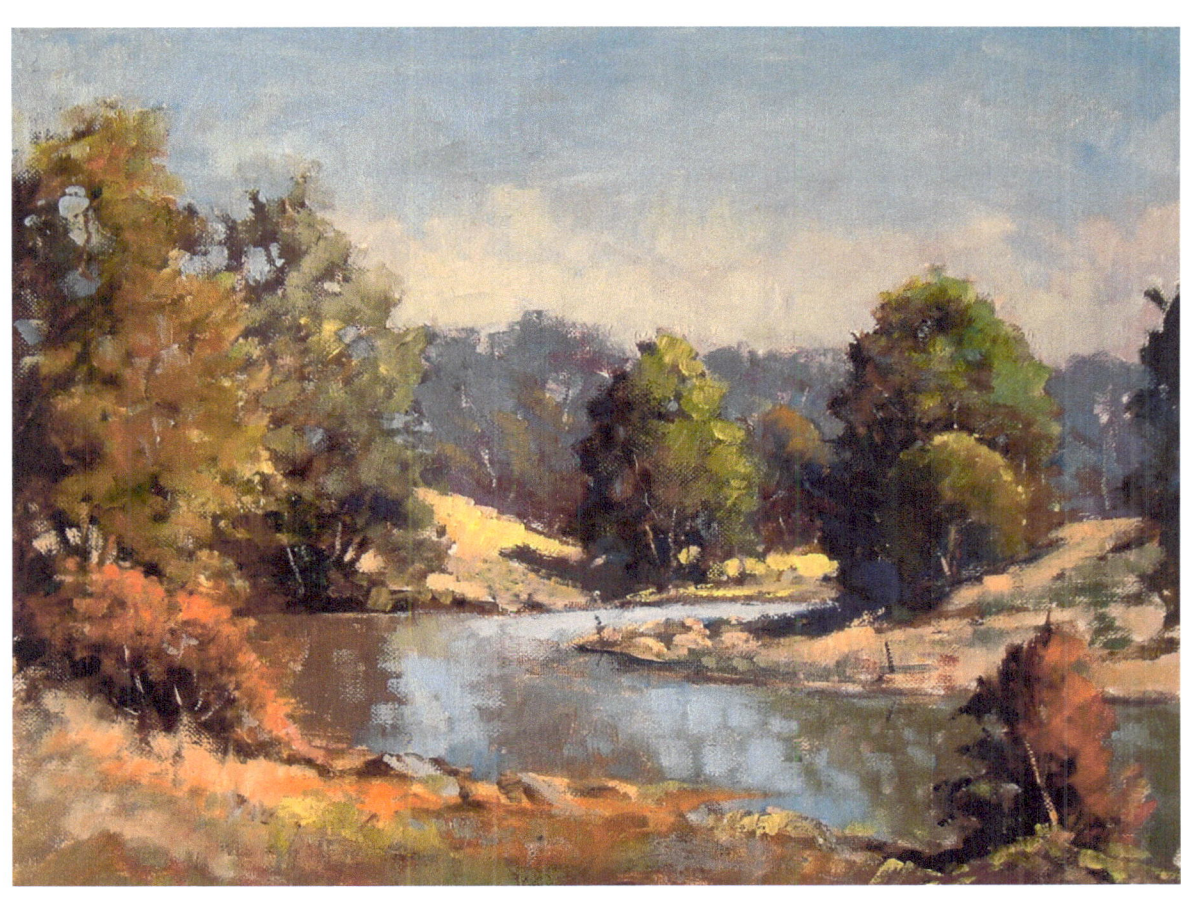

Hastings Point, NSW

Warrambungles

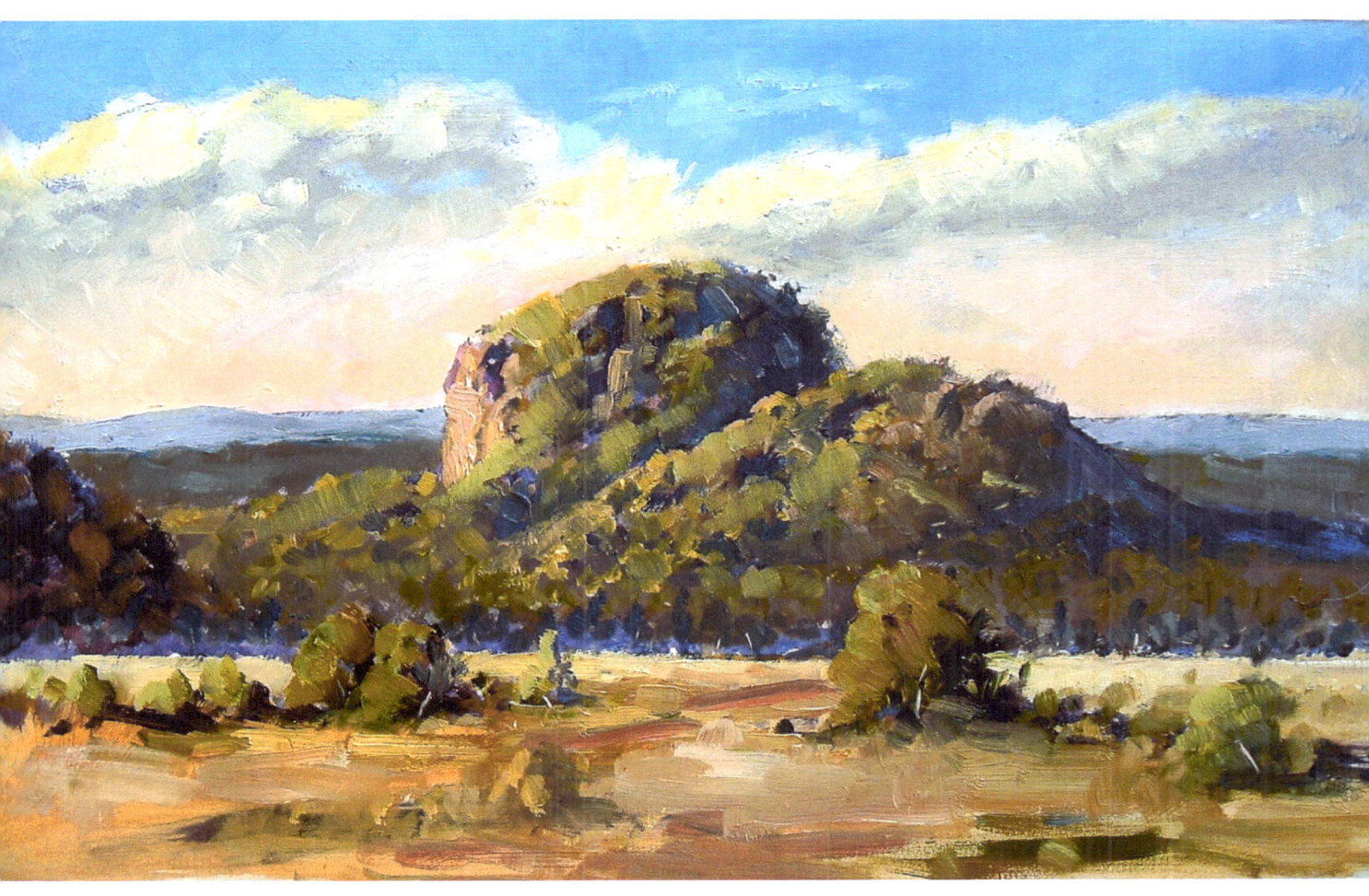

The Border Ranges, NSW

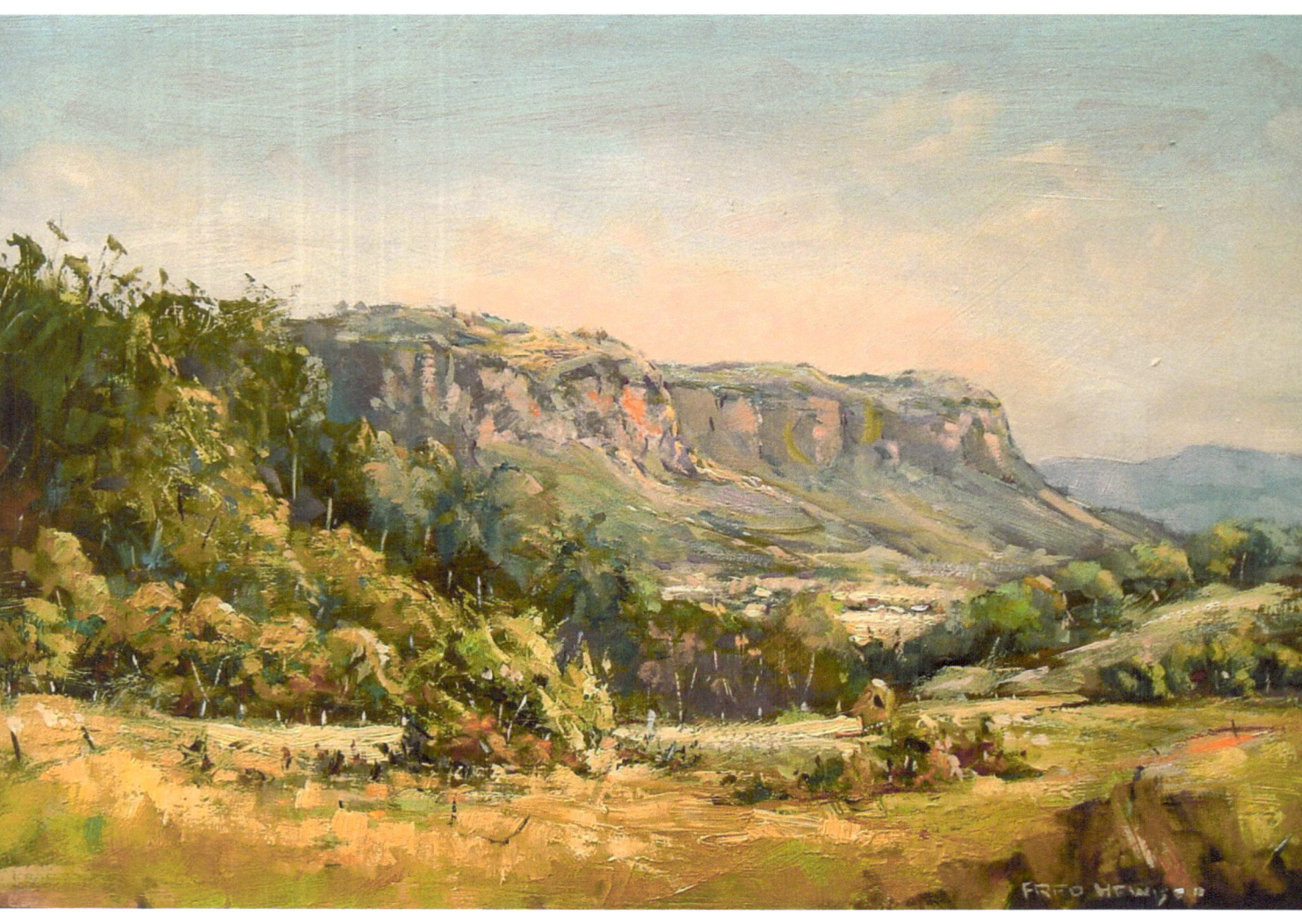

Tweed River

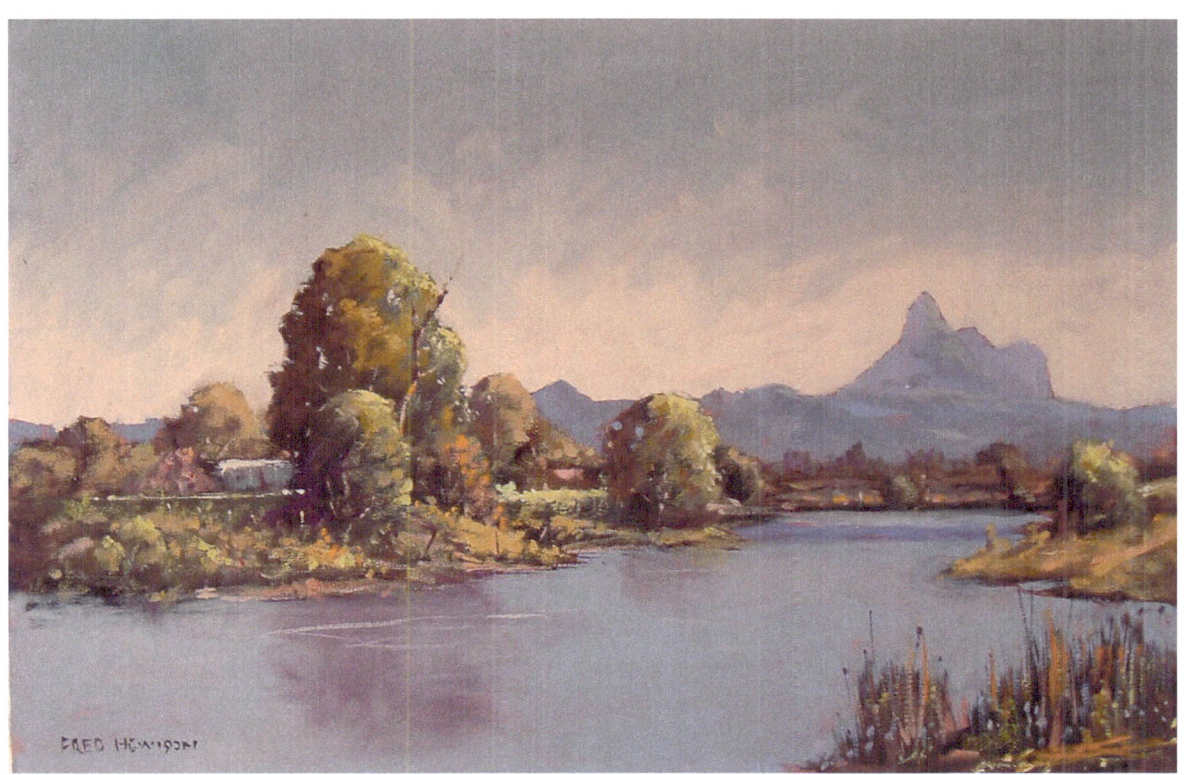

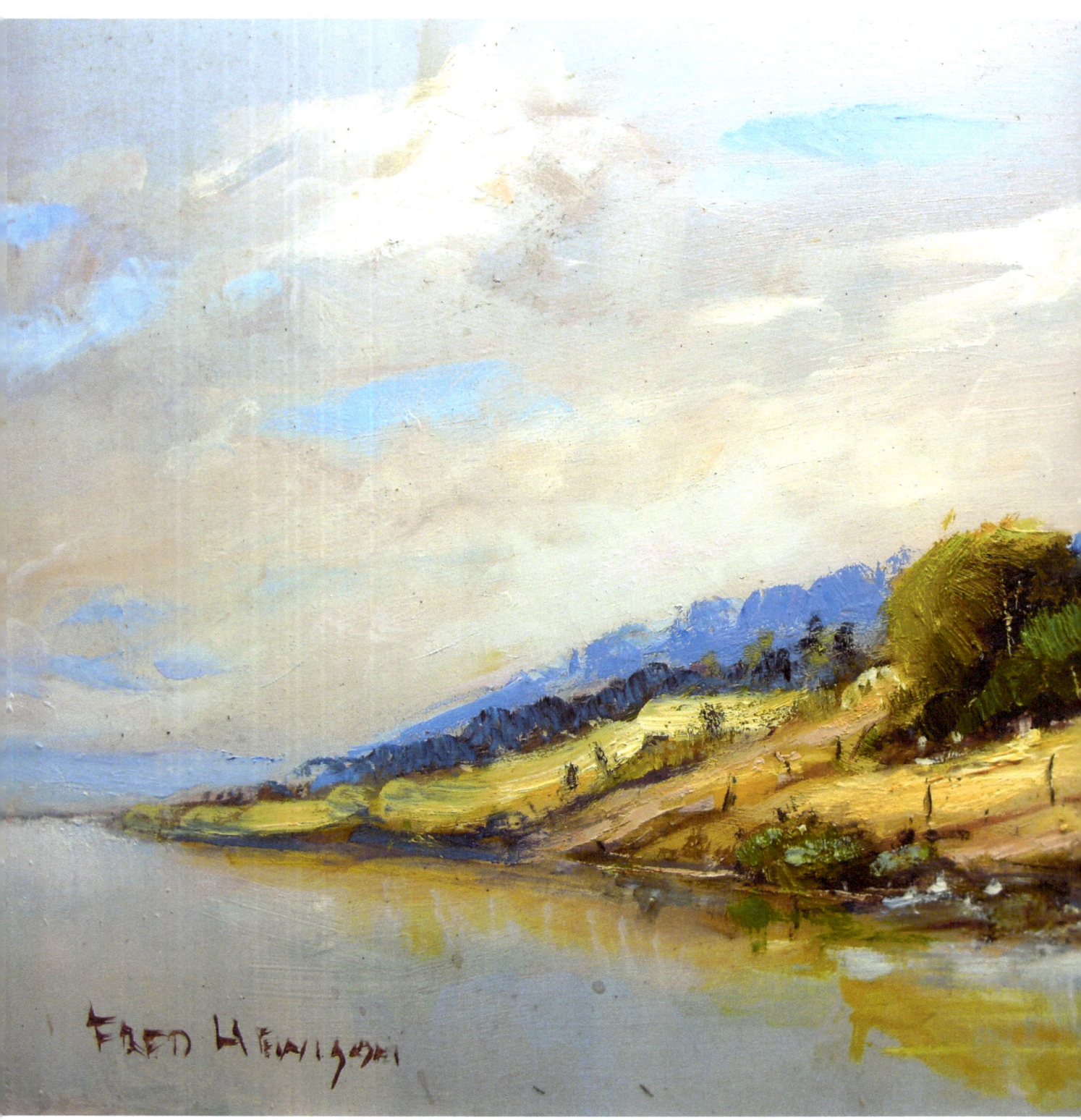

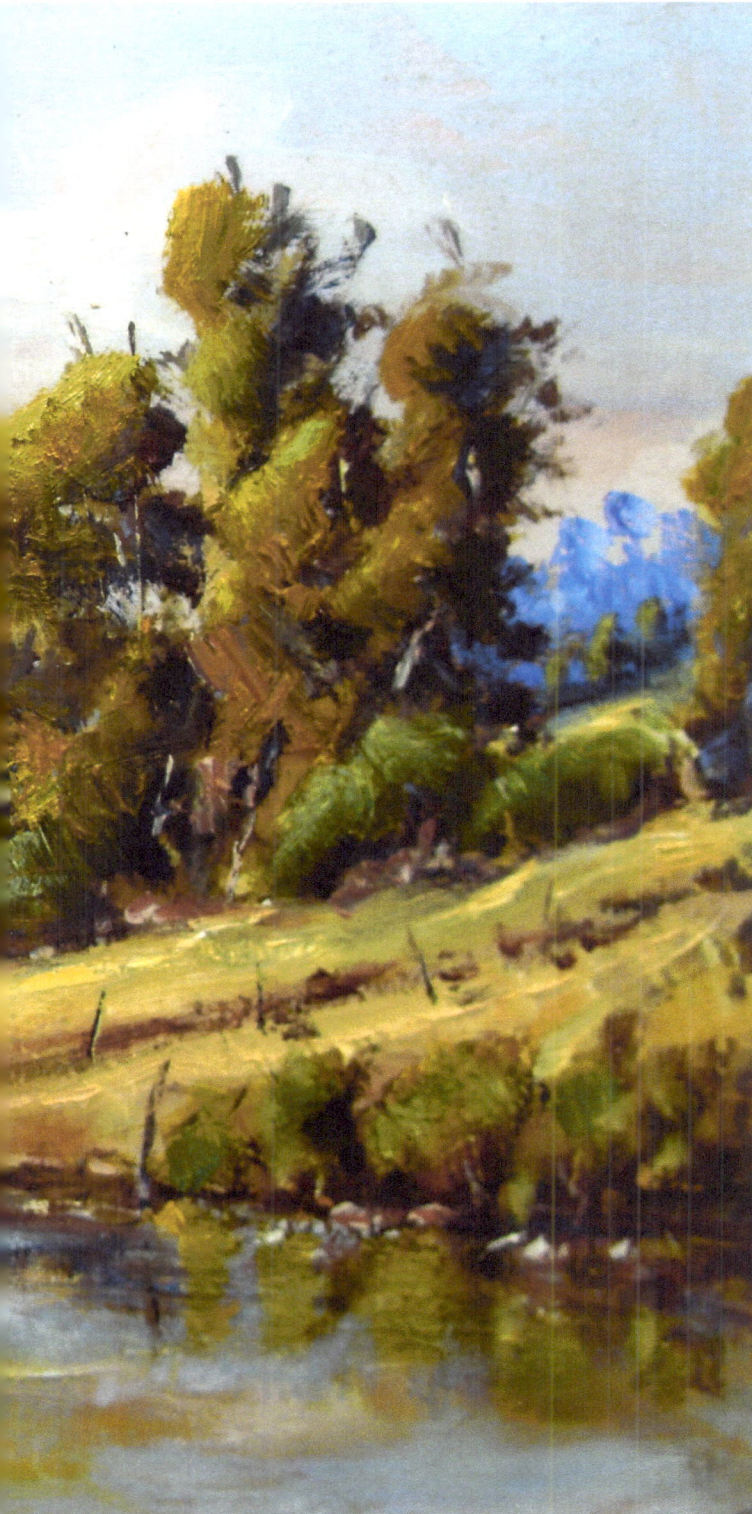

Edge of the Lake

Eucalyptus

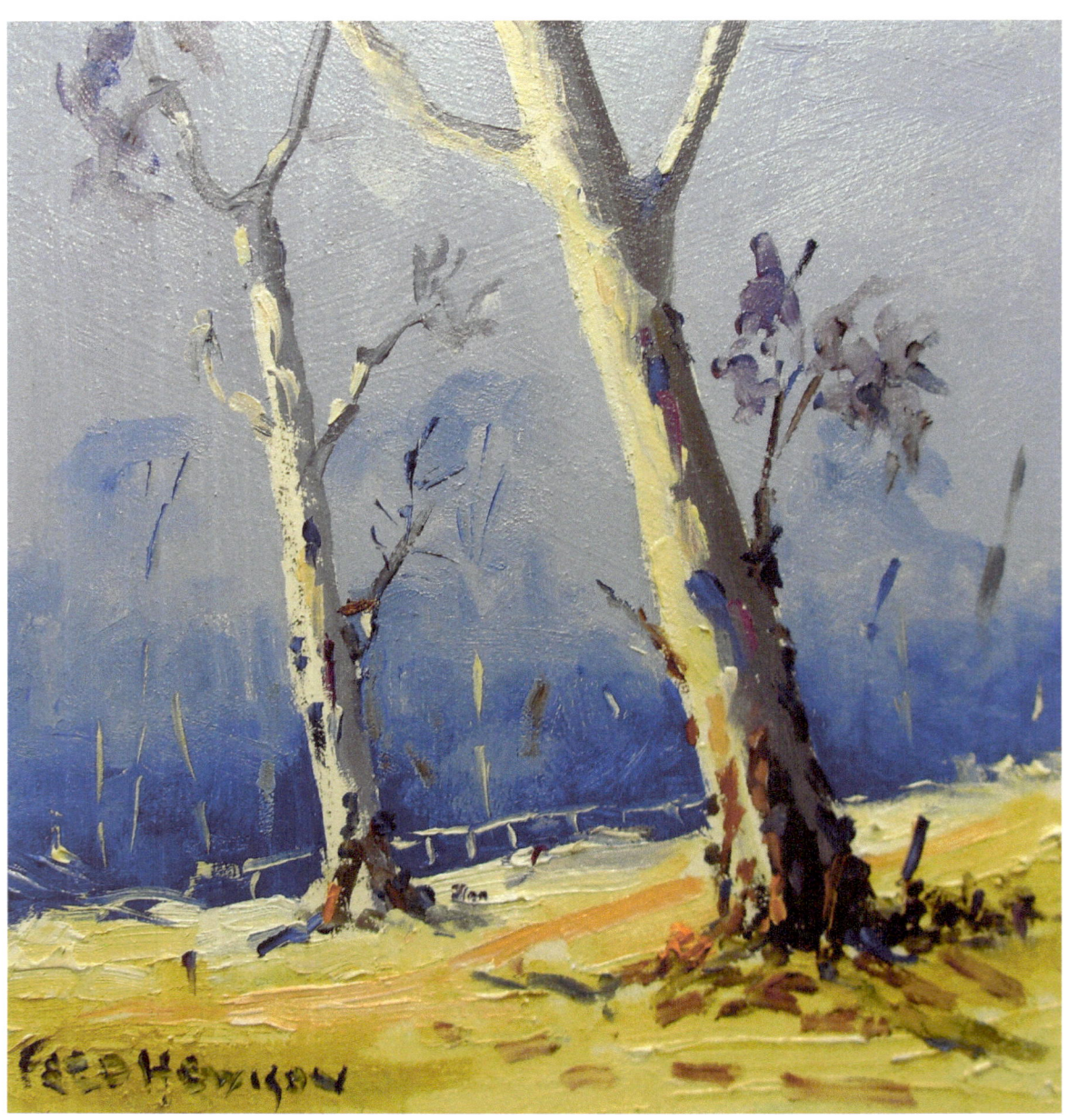

Late Afternoon, Grafton

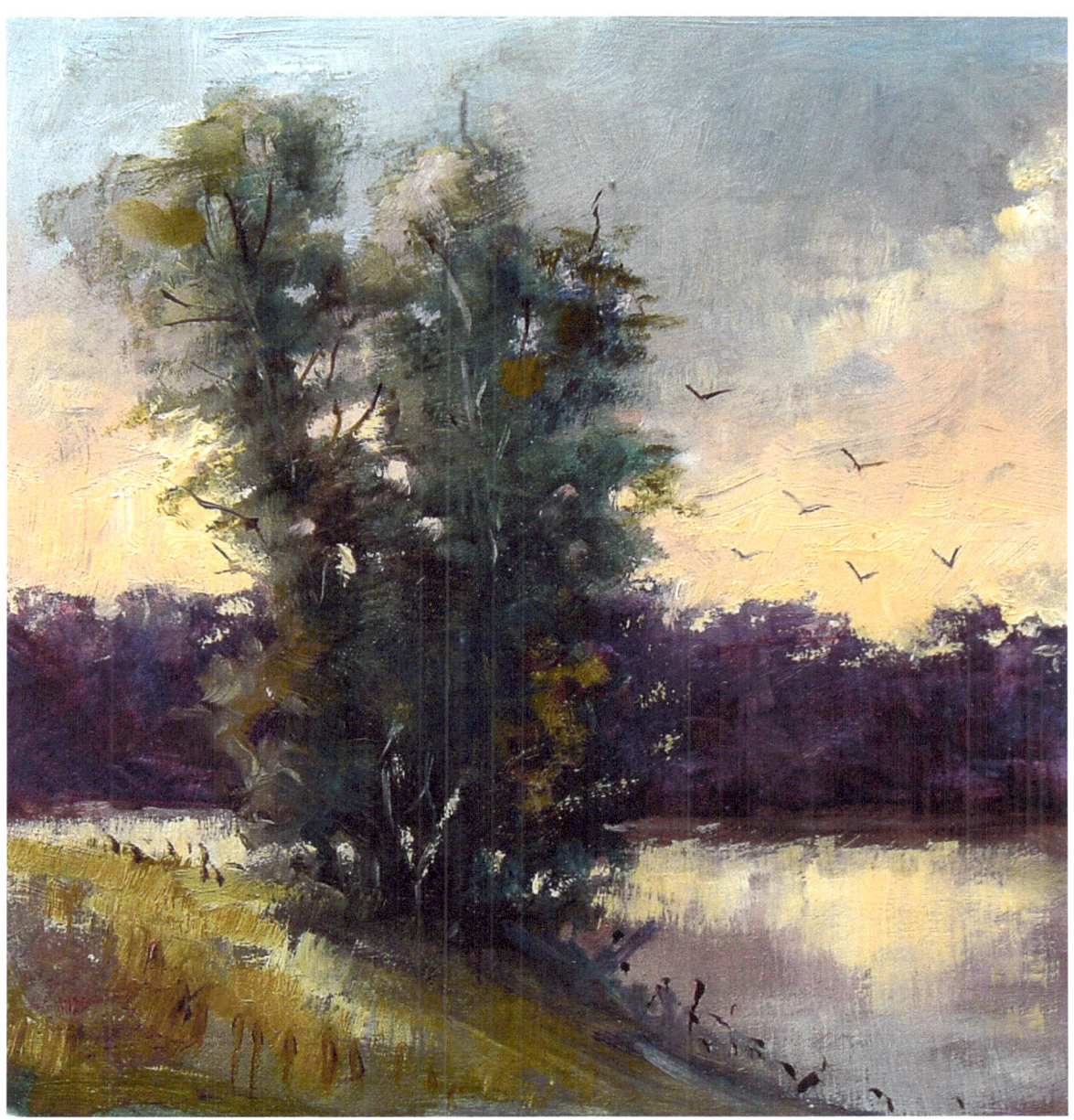

Fisherman Friend, Neil

Tumbulgum

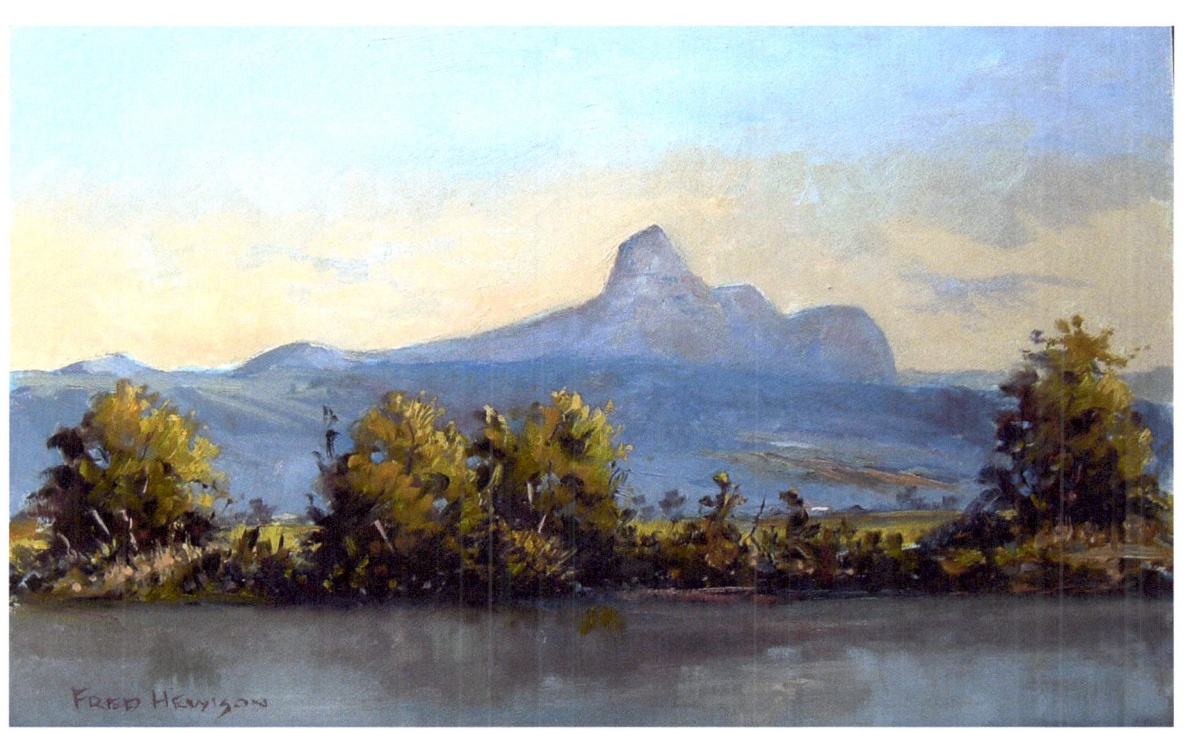

Bray Park, NSW

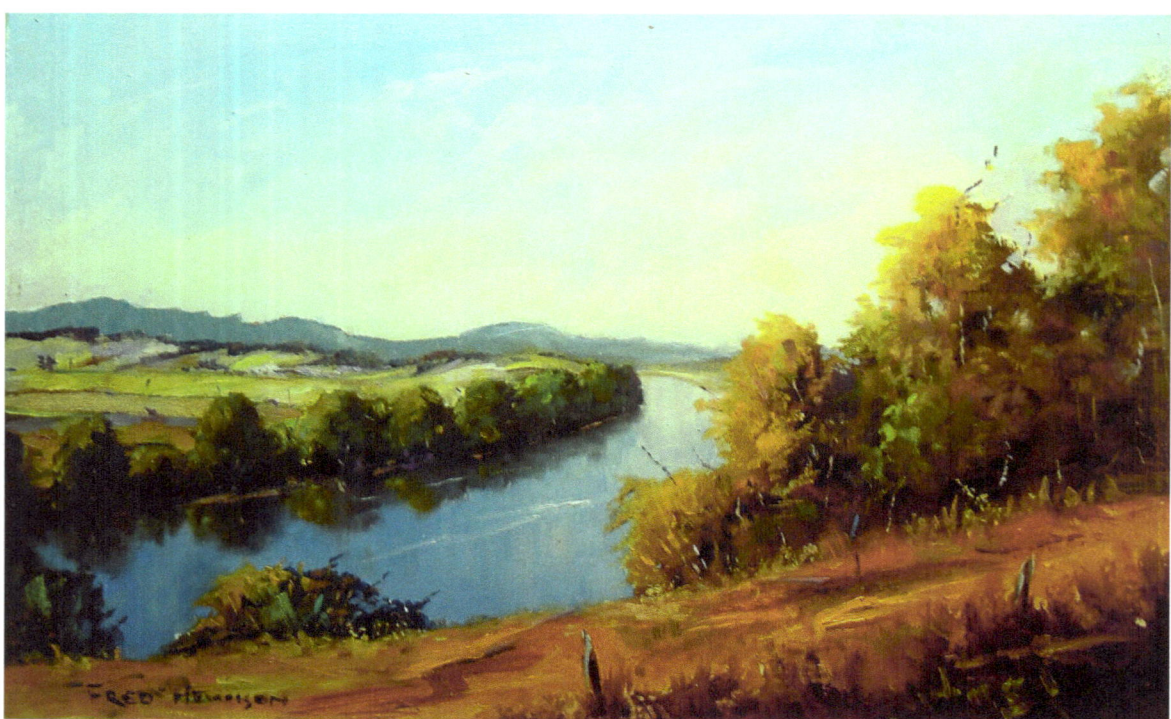

Tweed River

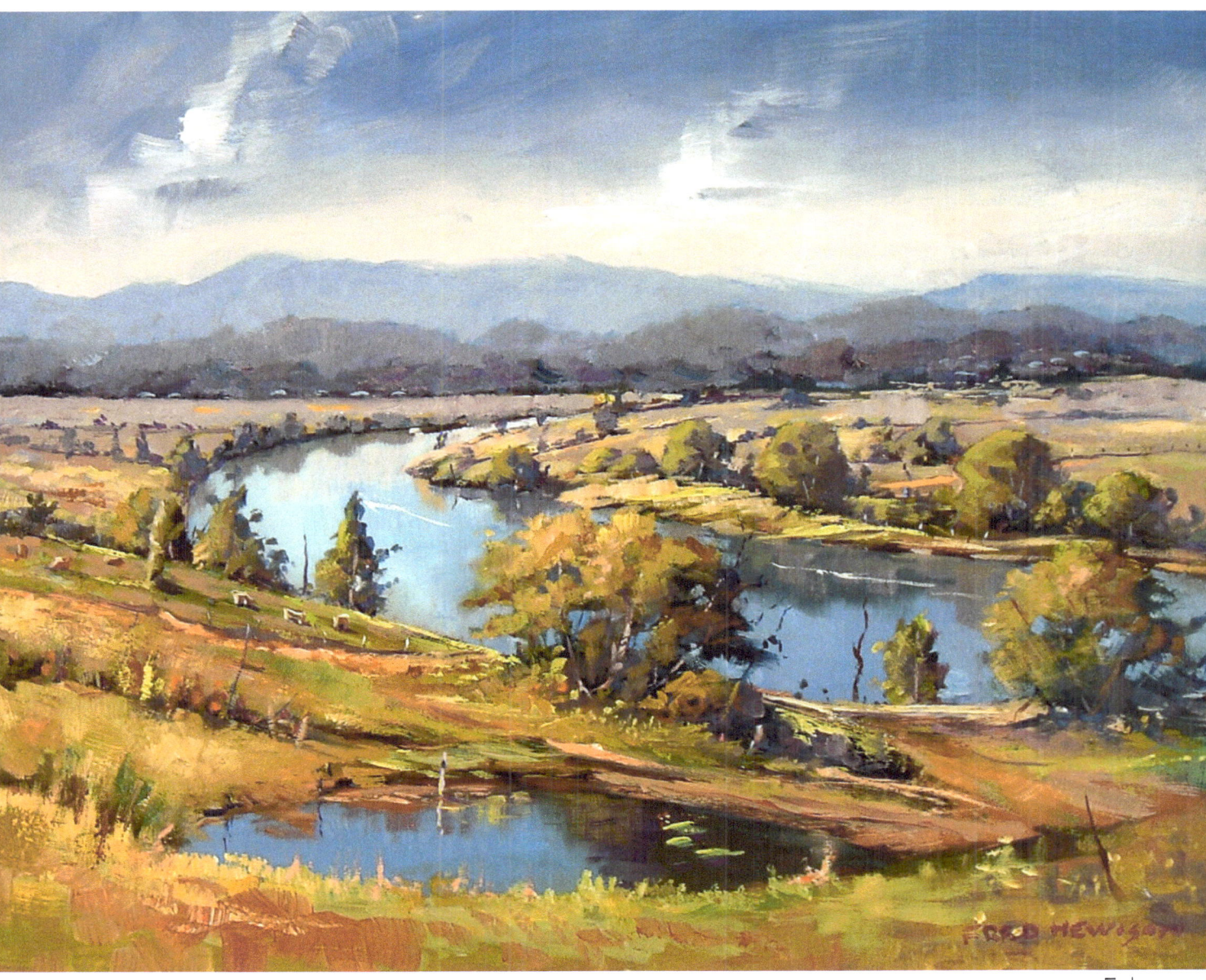

Tweed River

Towards the Border Ranges

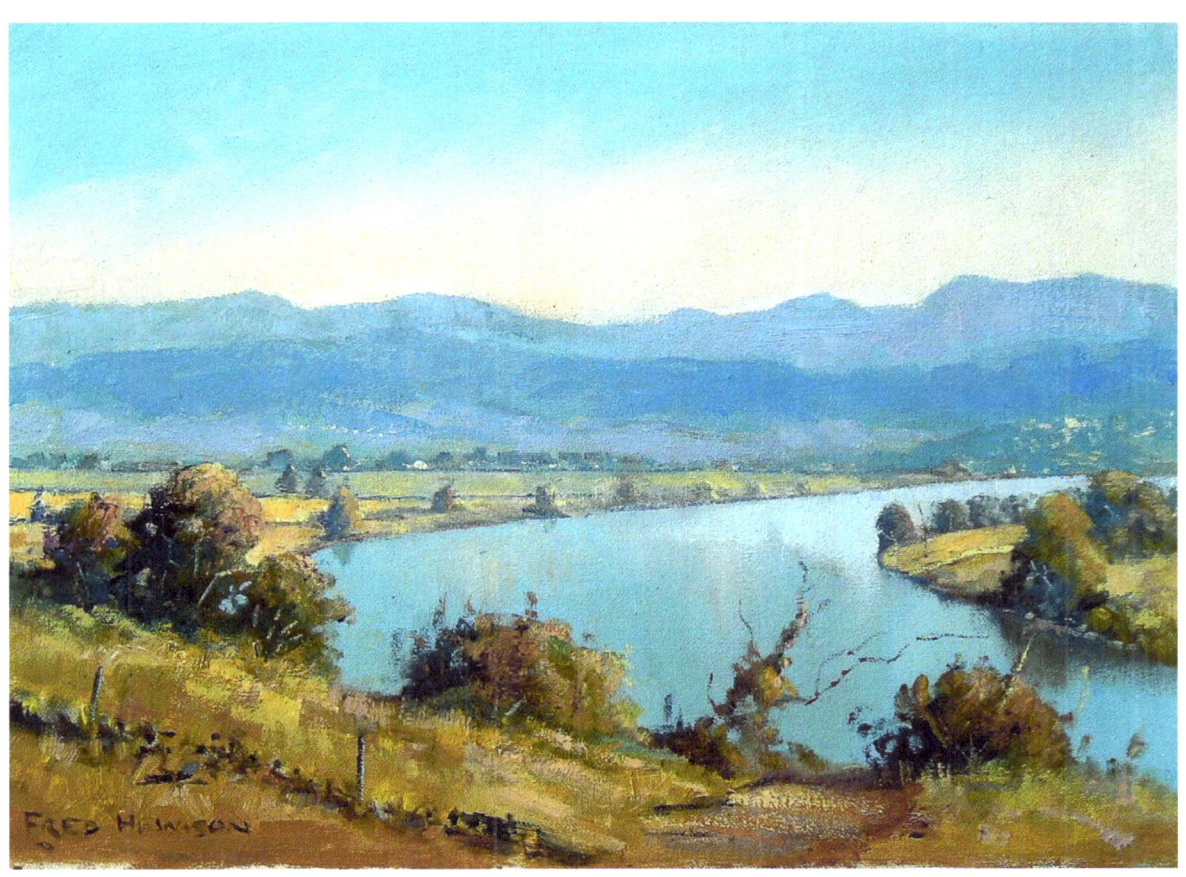

A place to Rest

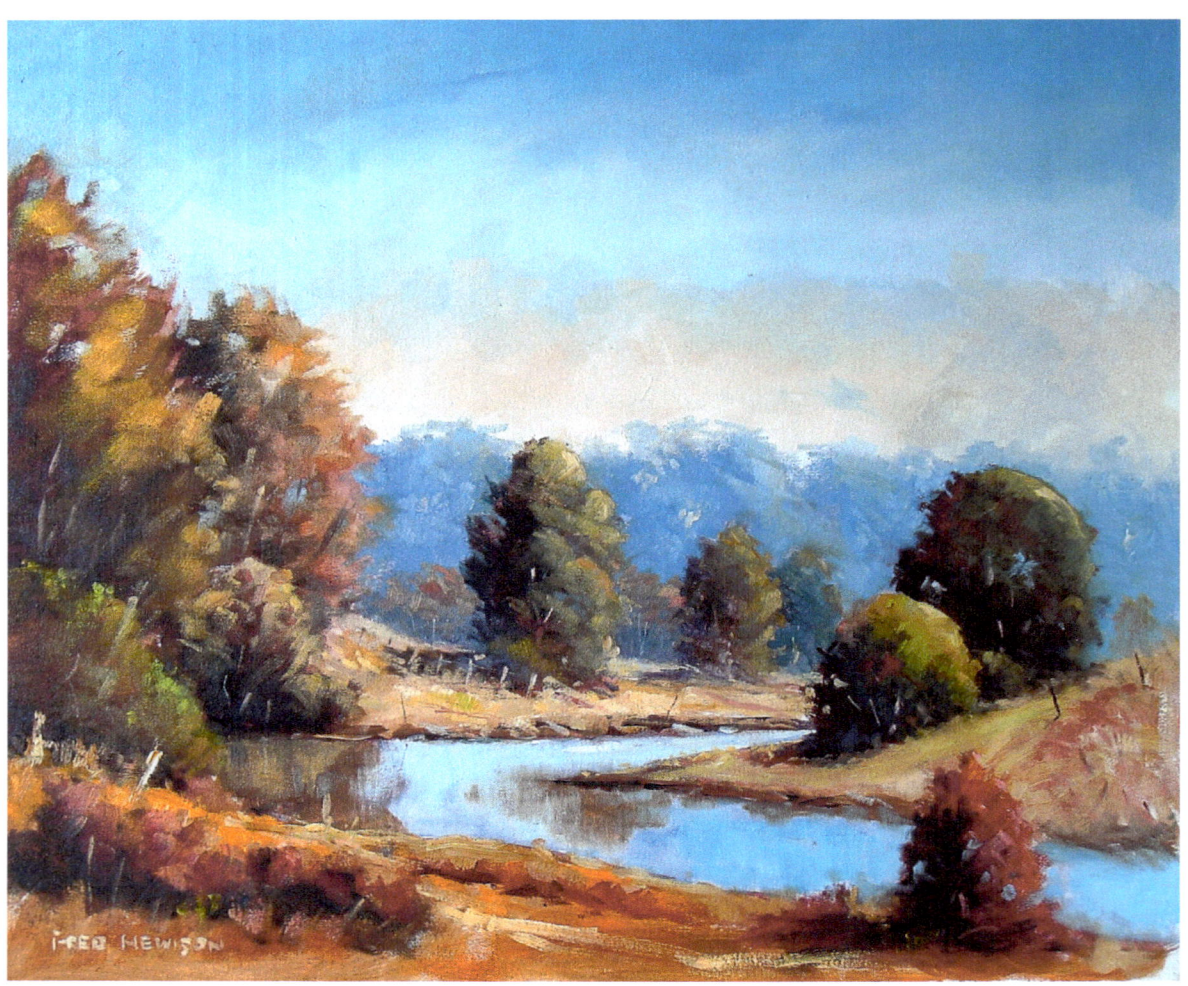

Tweed Terrarora

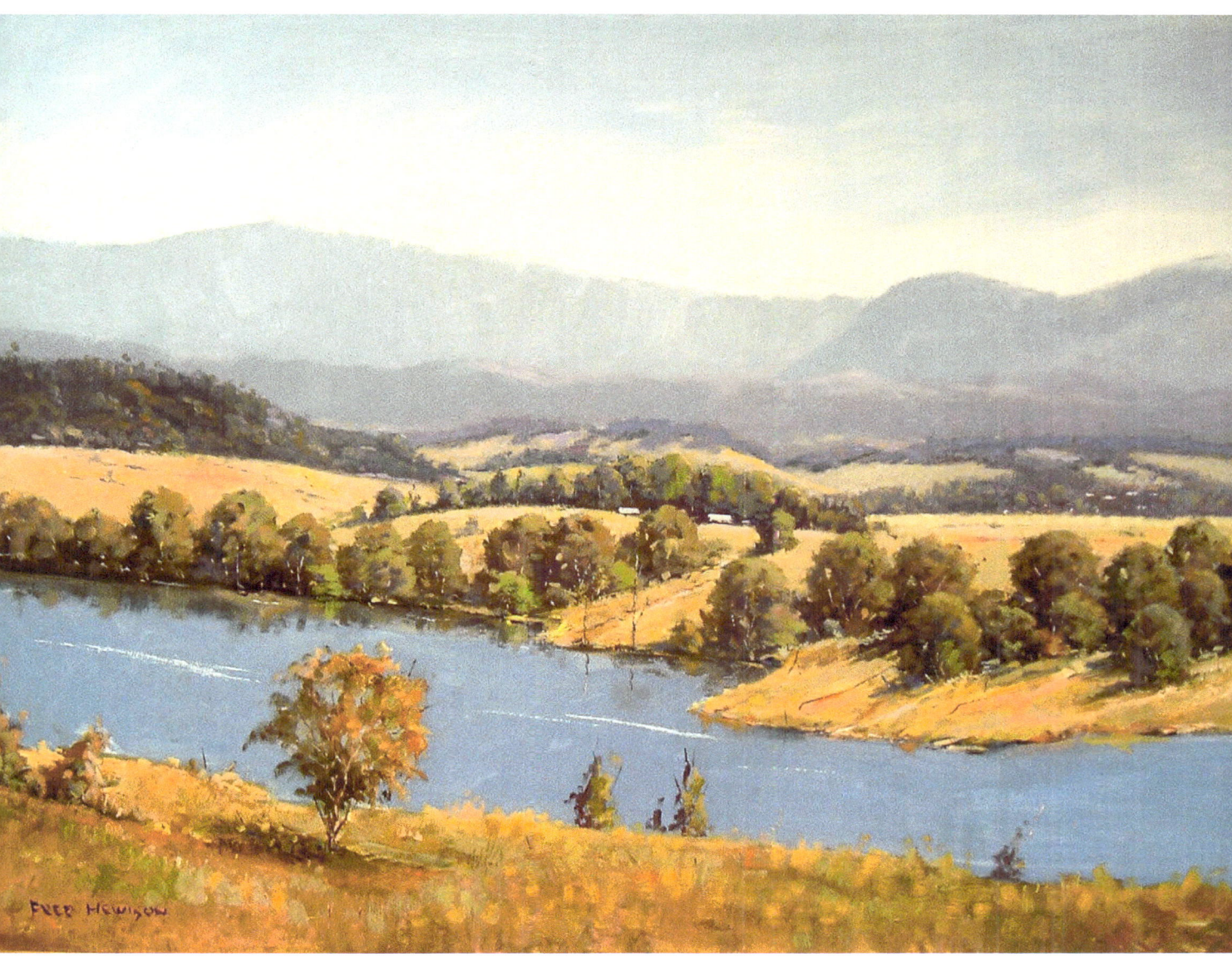

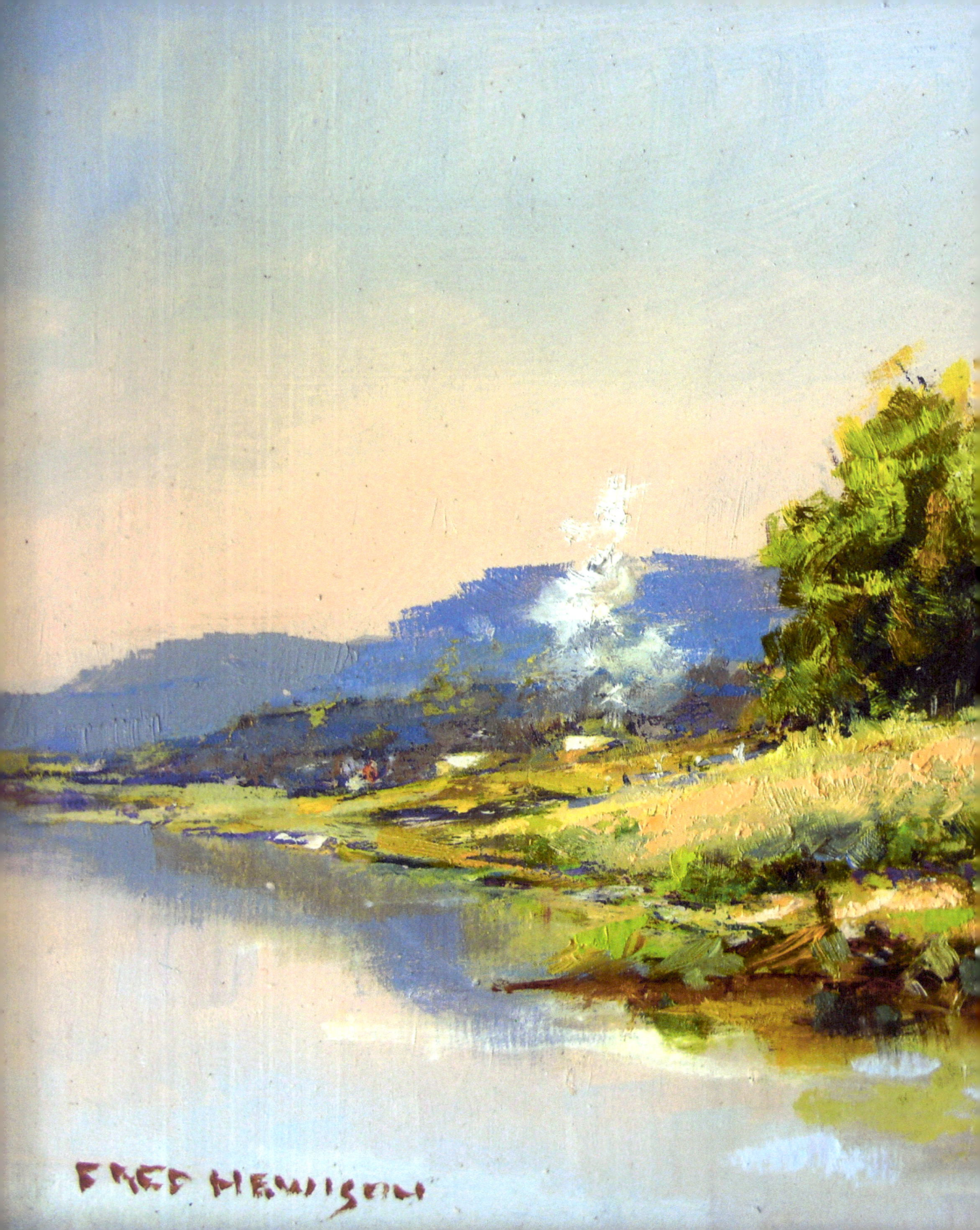

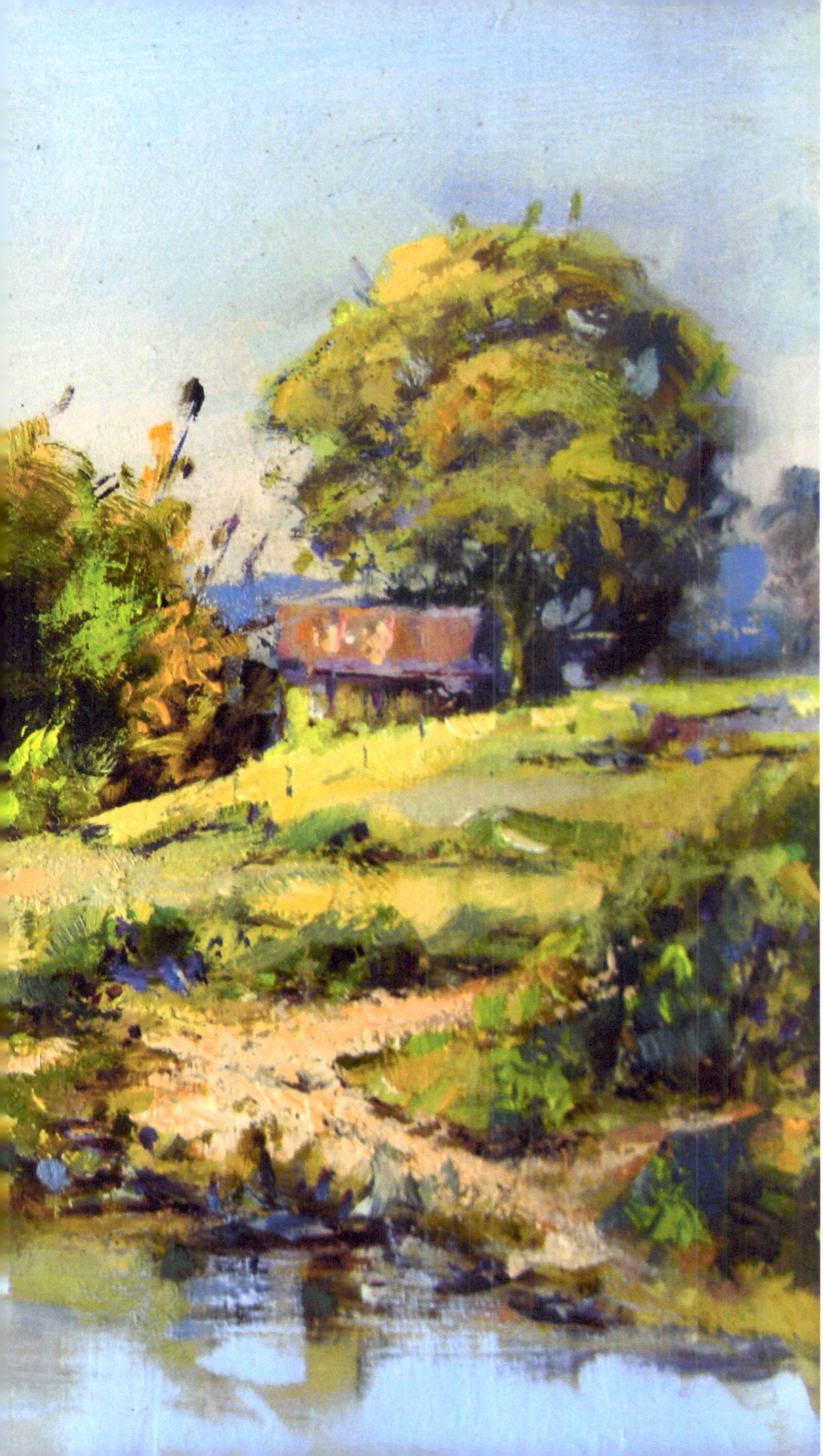

Shack by the Lake

Macintyre River, Inverell

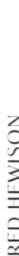

Reflections, Copmanhurst

Grose Valley, Blue Mountains

The Three Sisters, Blue Mountains

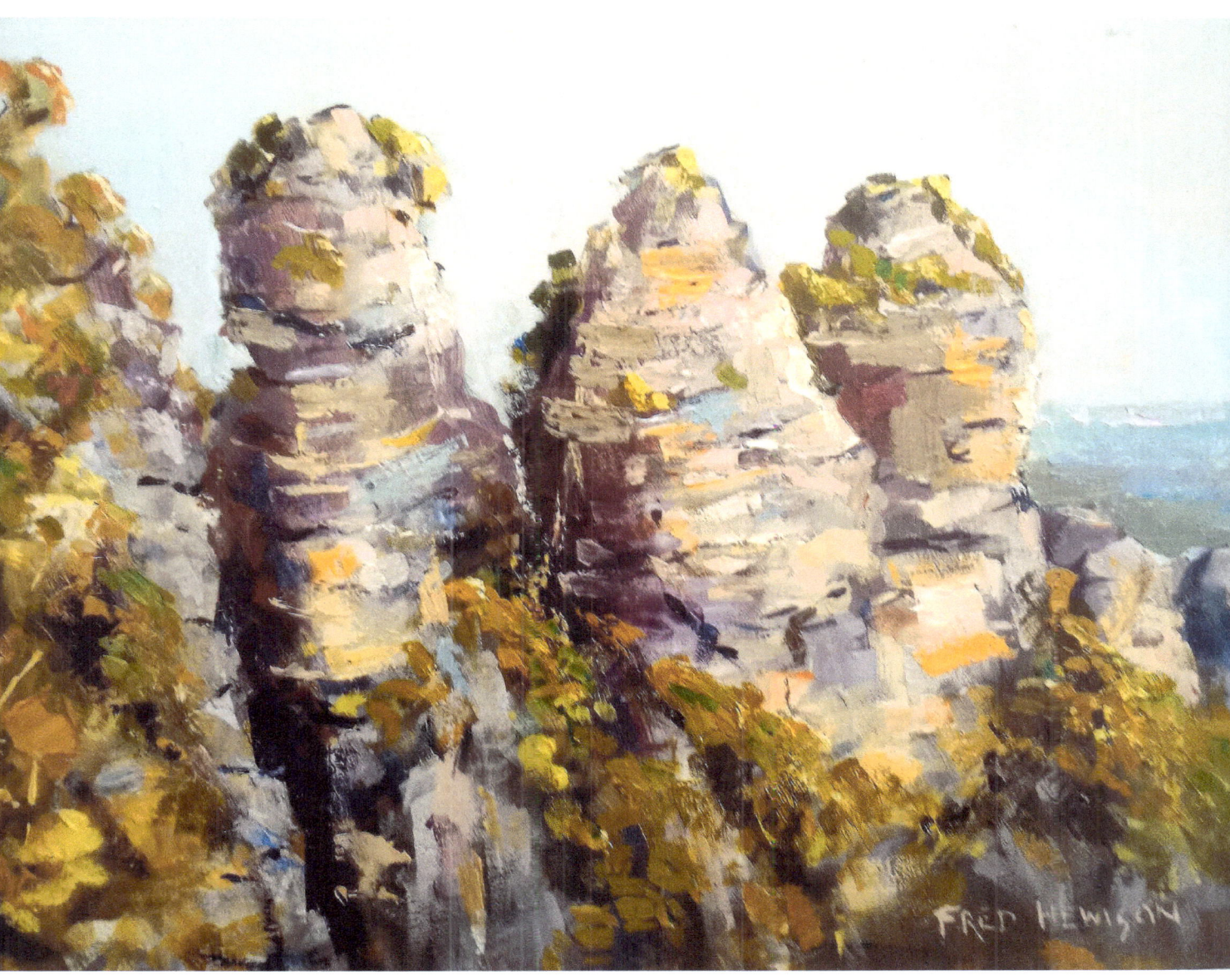

Two Gums

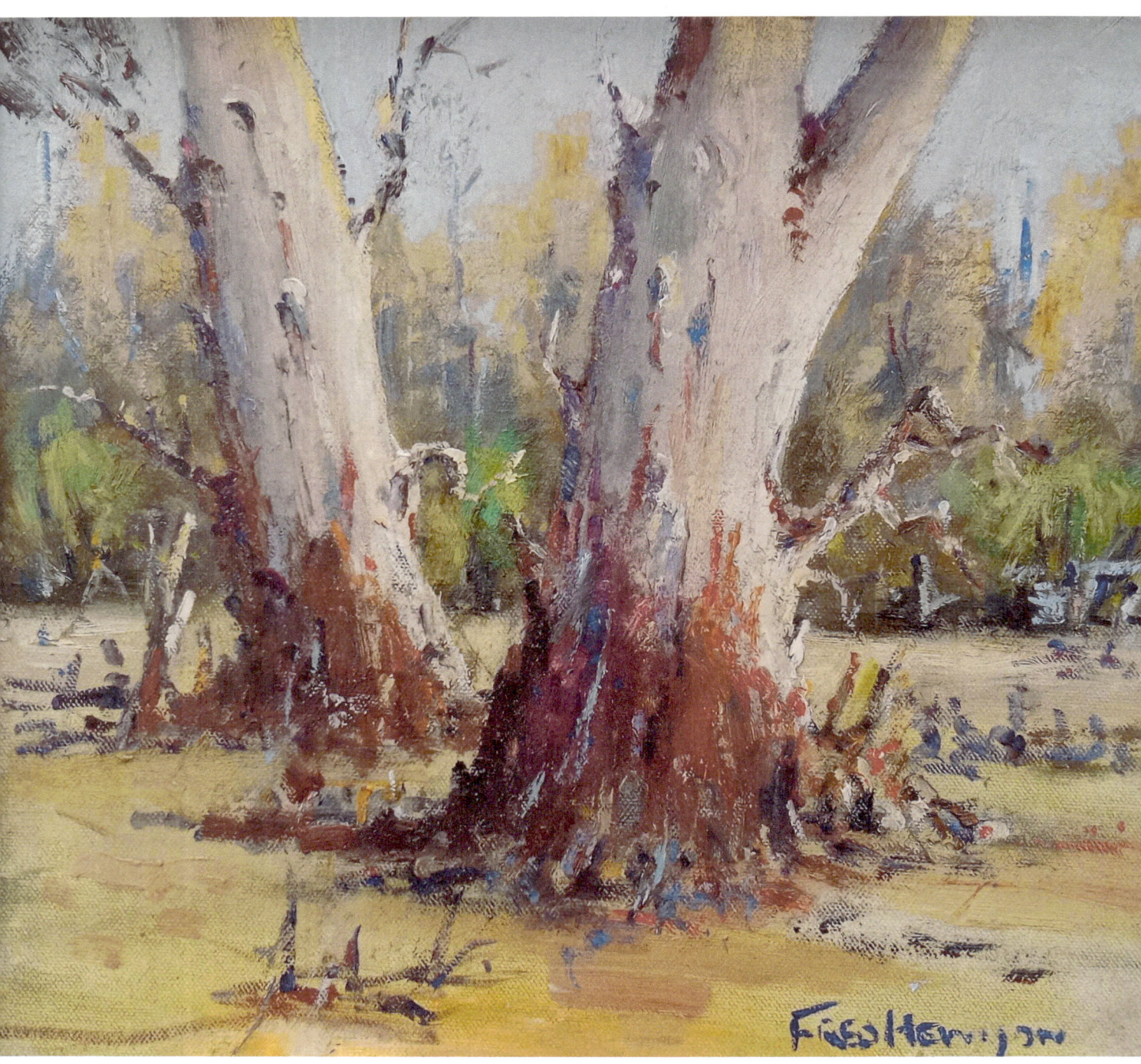

A Place to Cast a Line

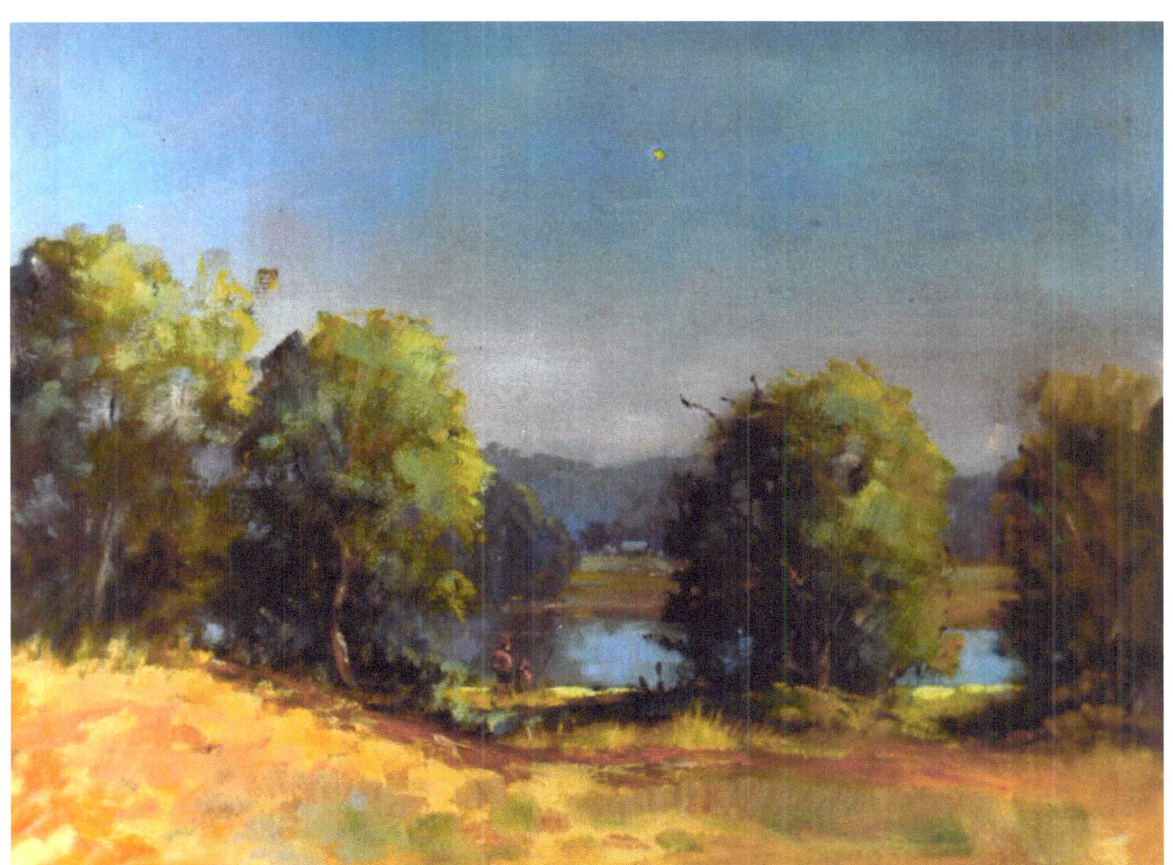

Early Morning

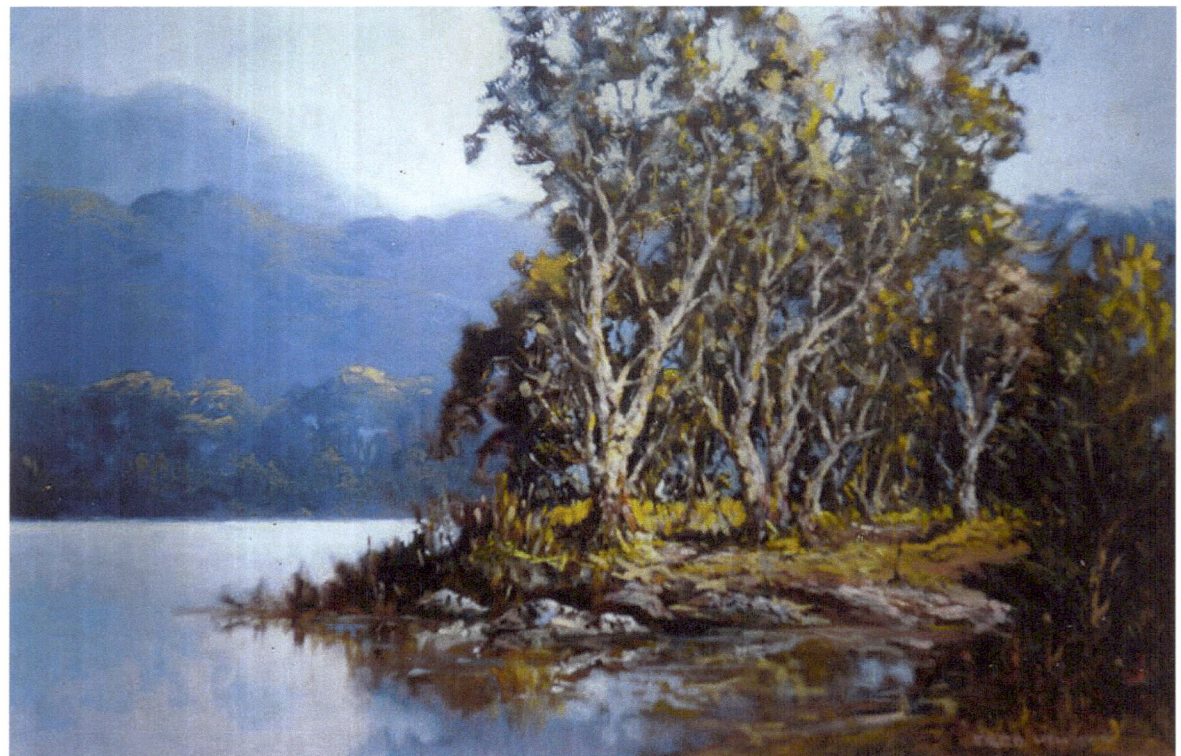

A Discussion

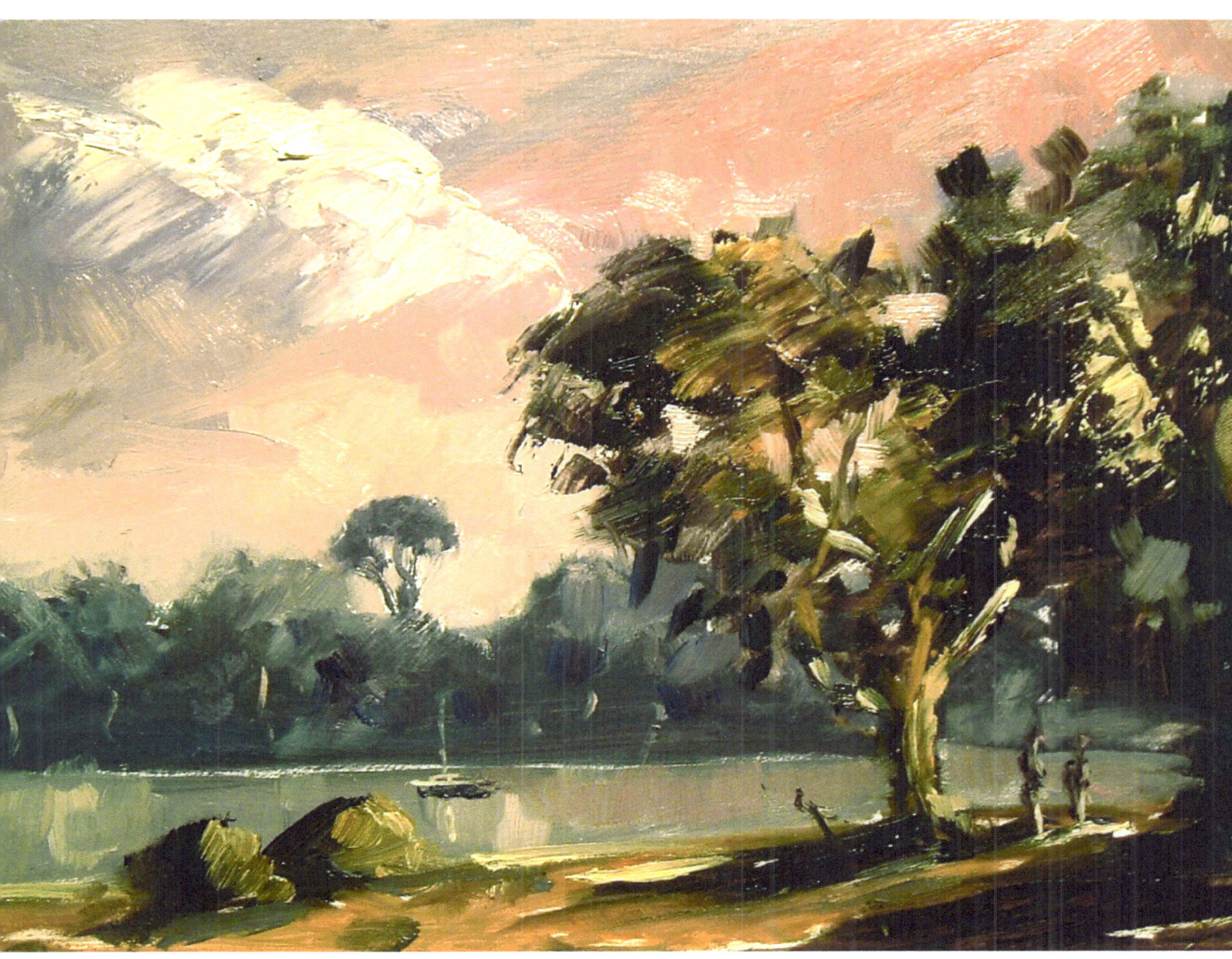

Near Griffith, NSW

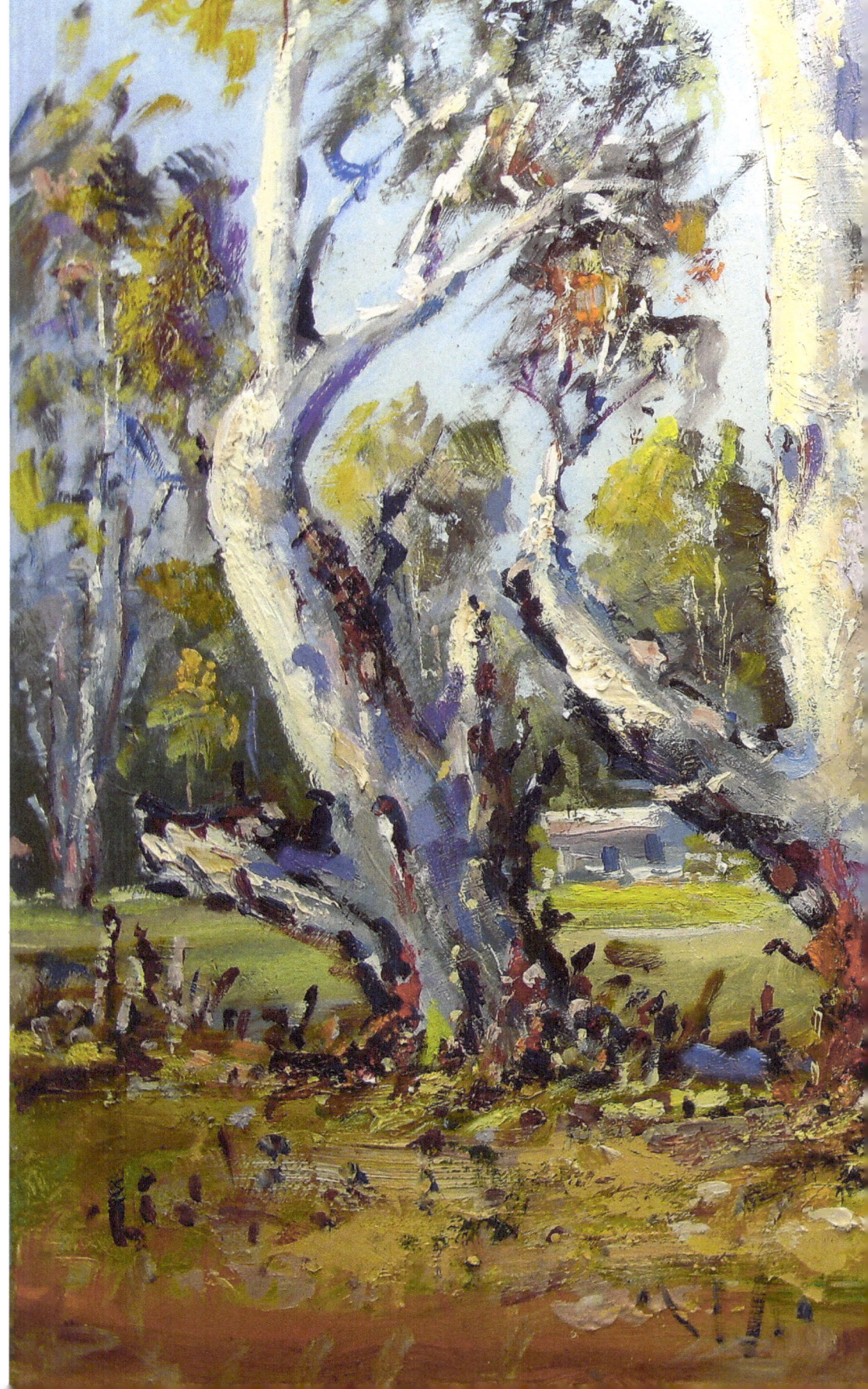

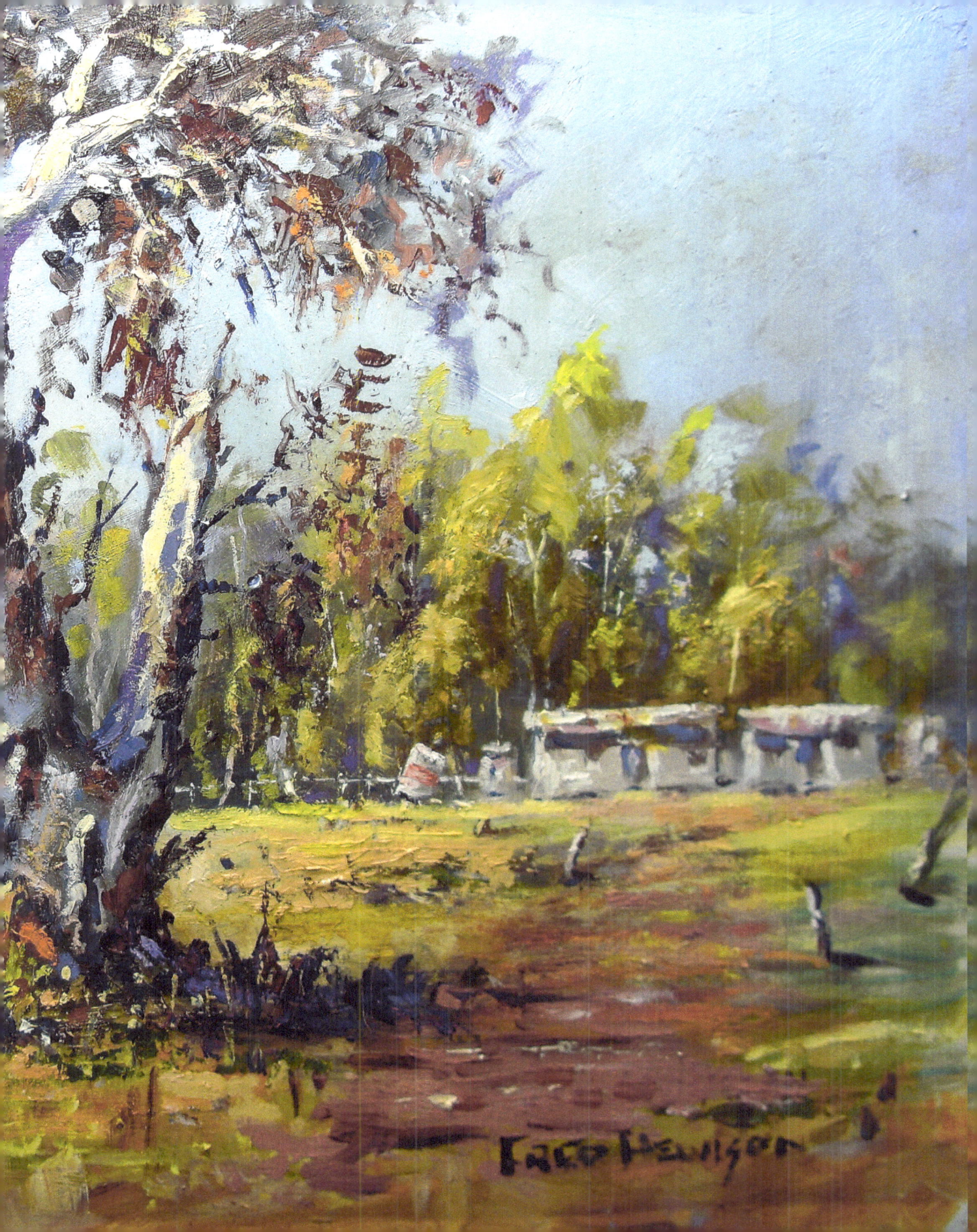

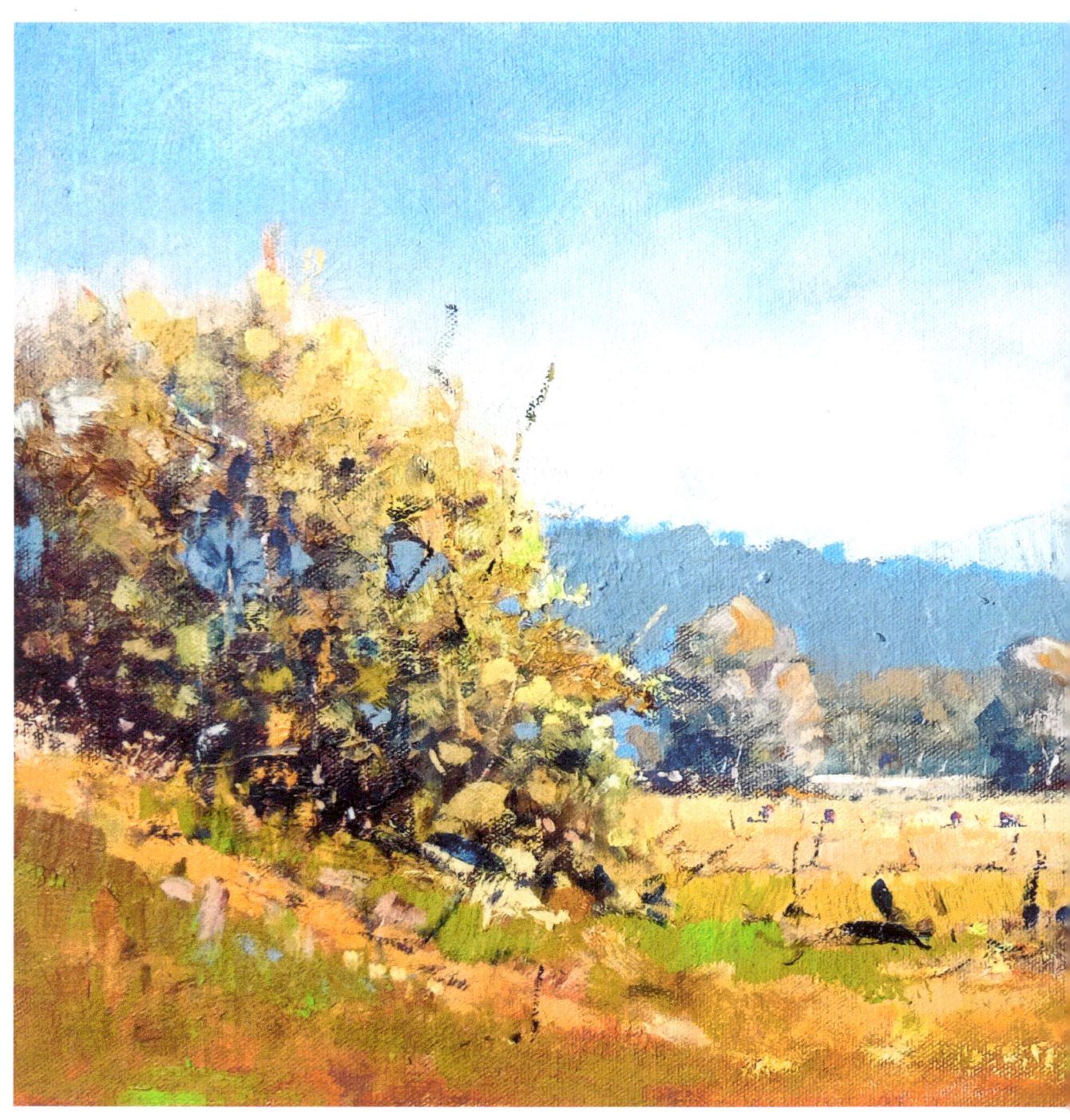

Summer

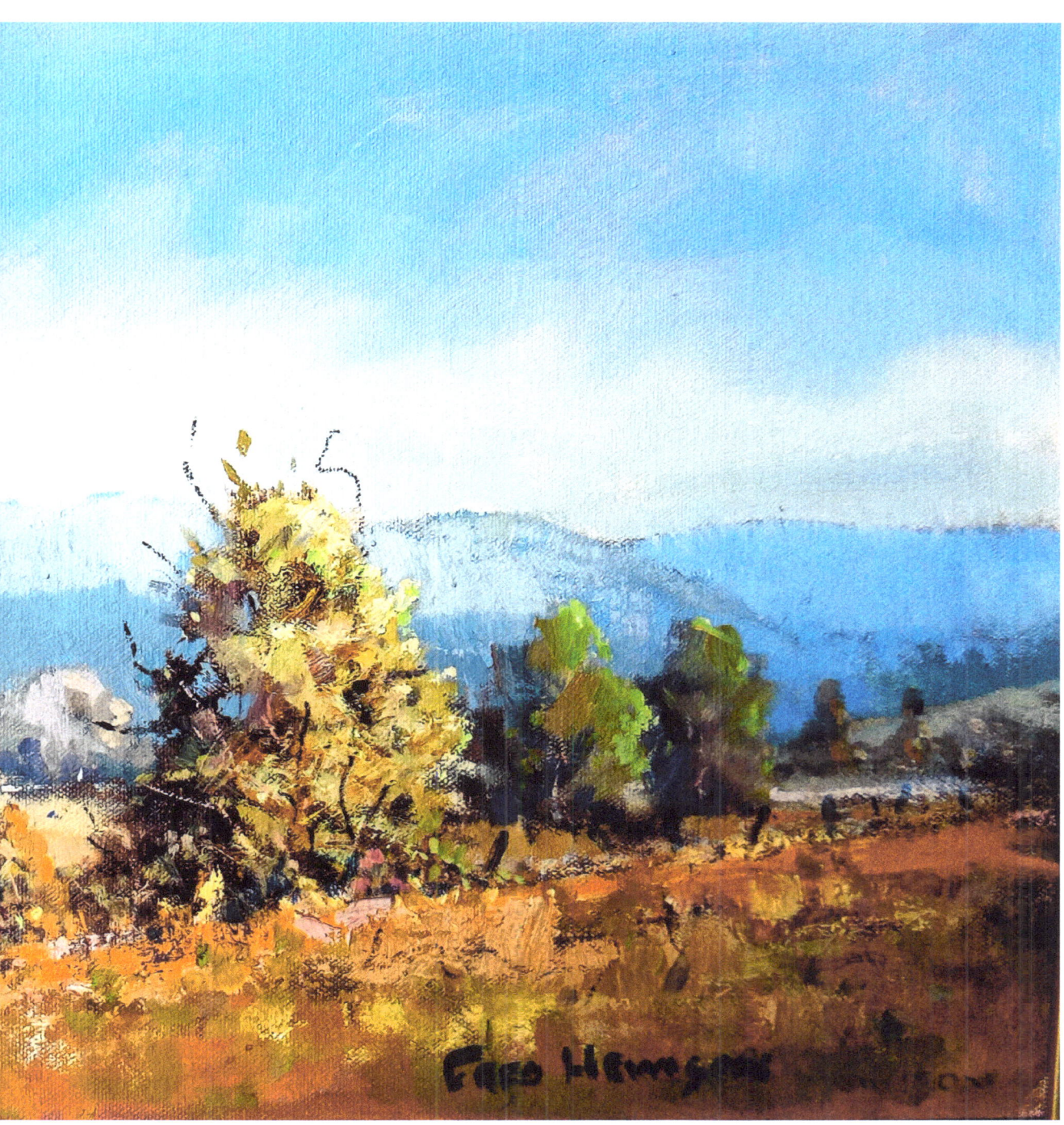

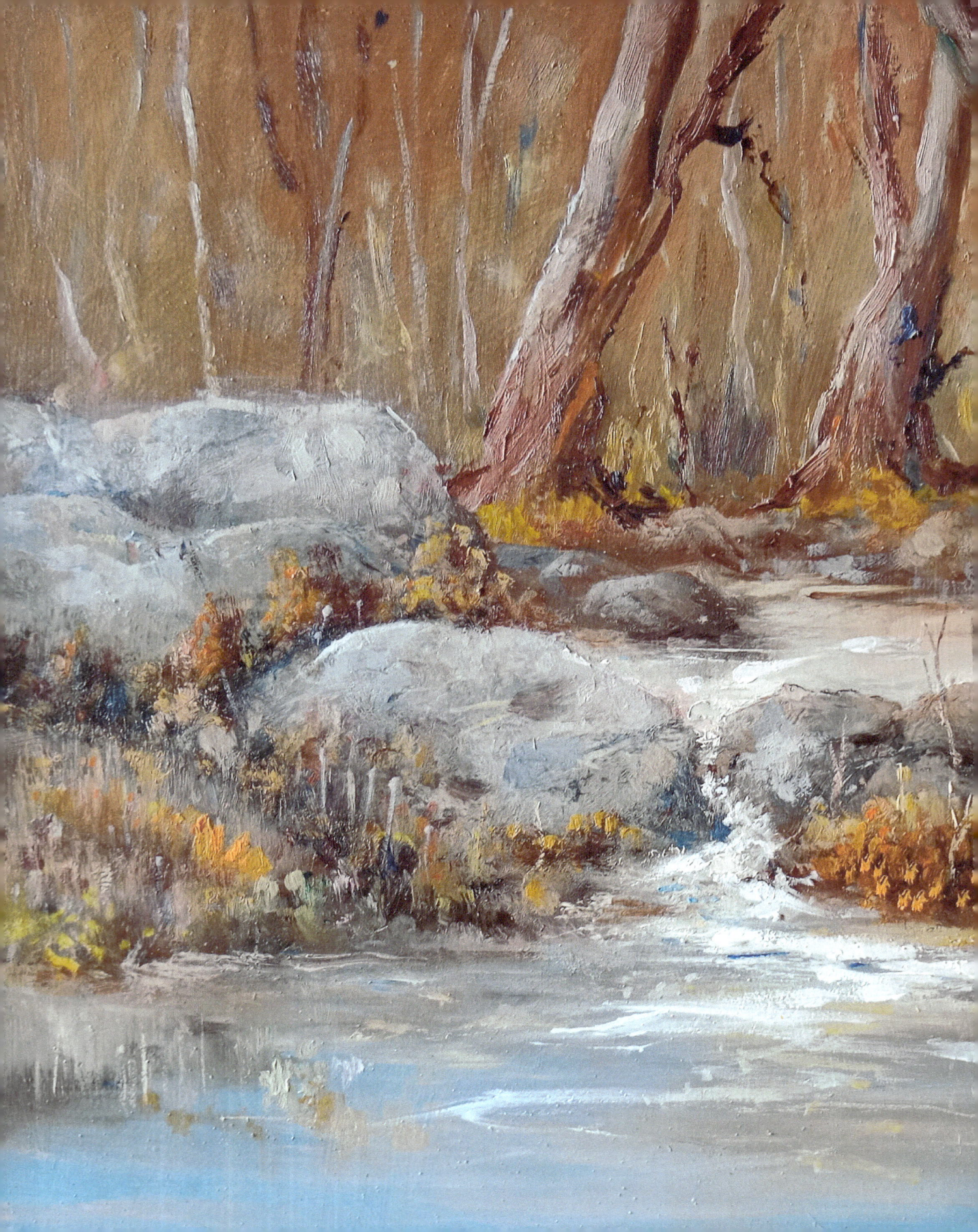

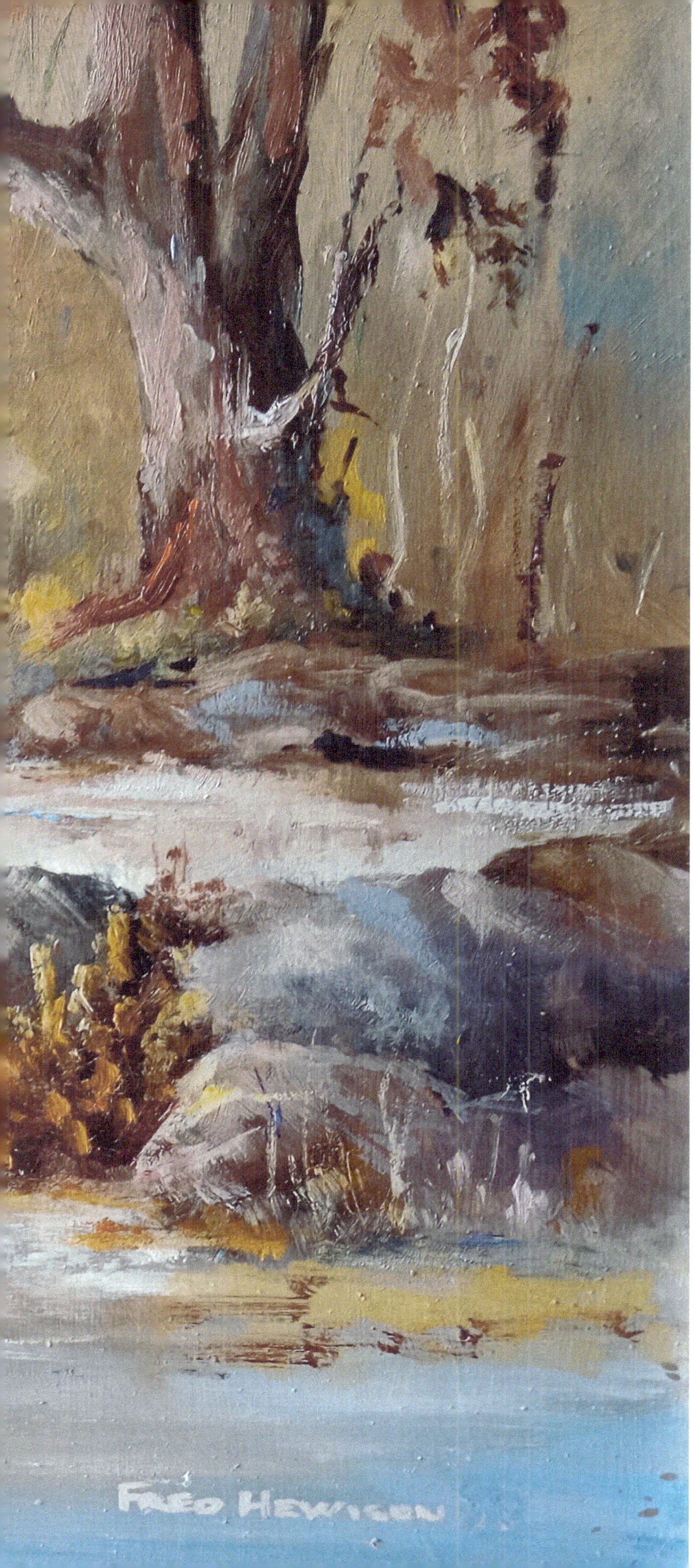

The Forest Pool

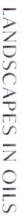

Casino, NSW

Evans Lookout, Blackheath, NSW

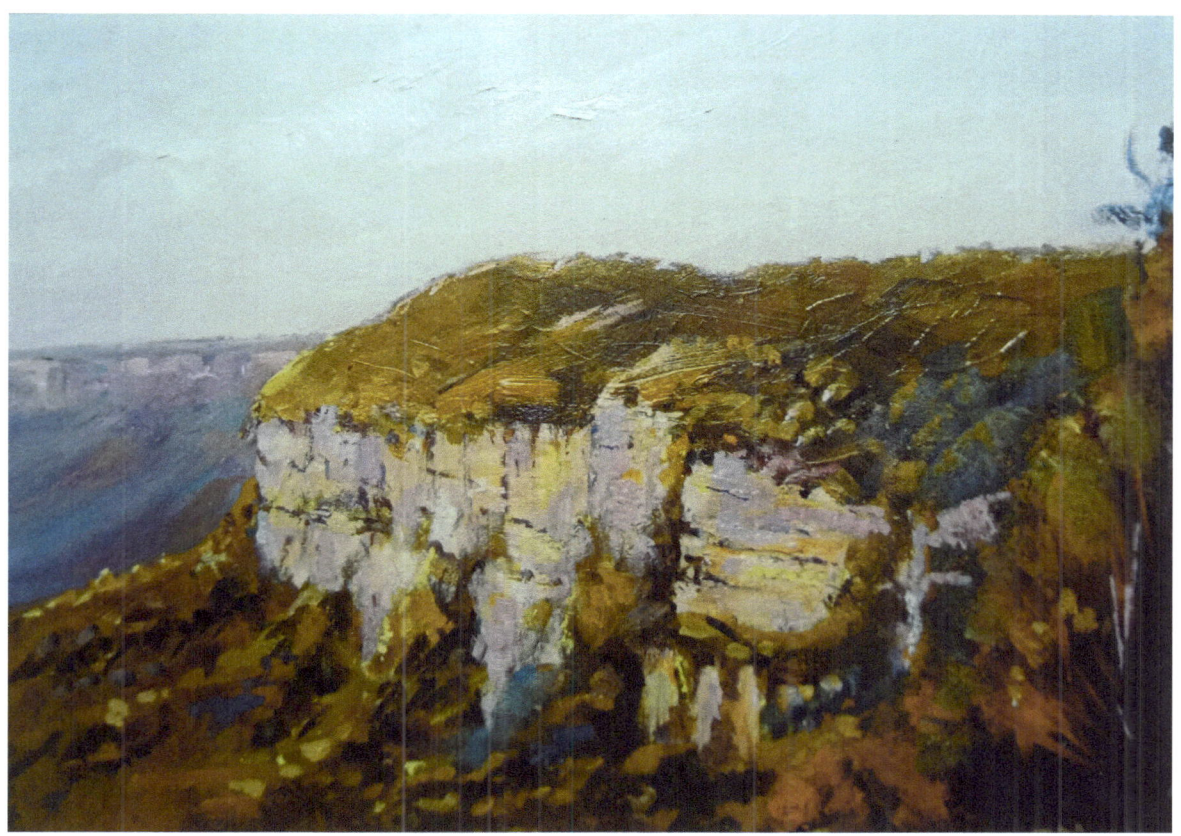

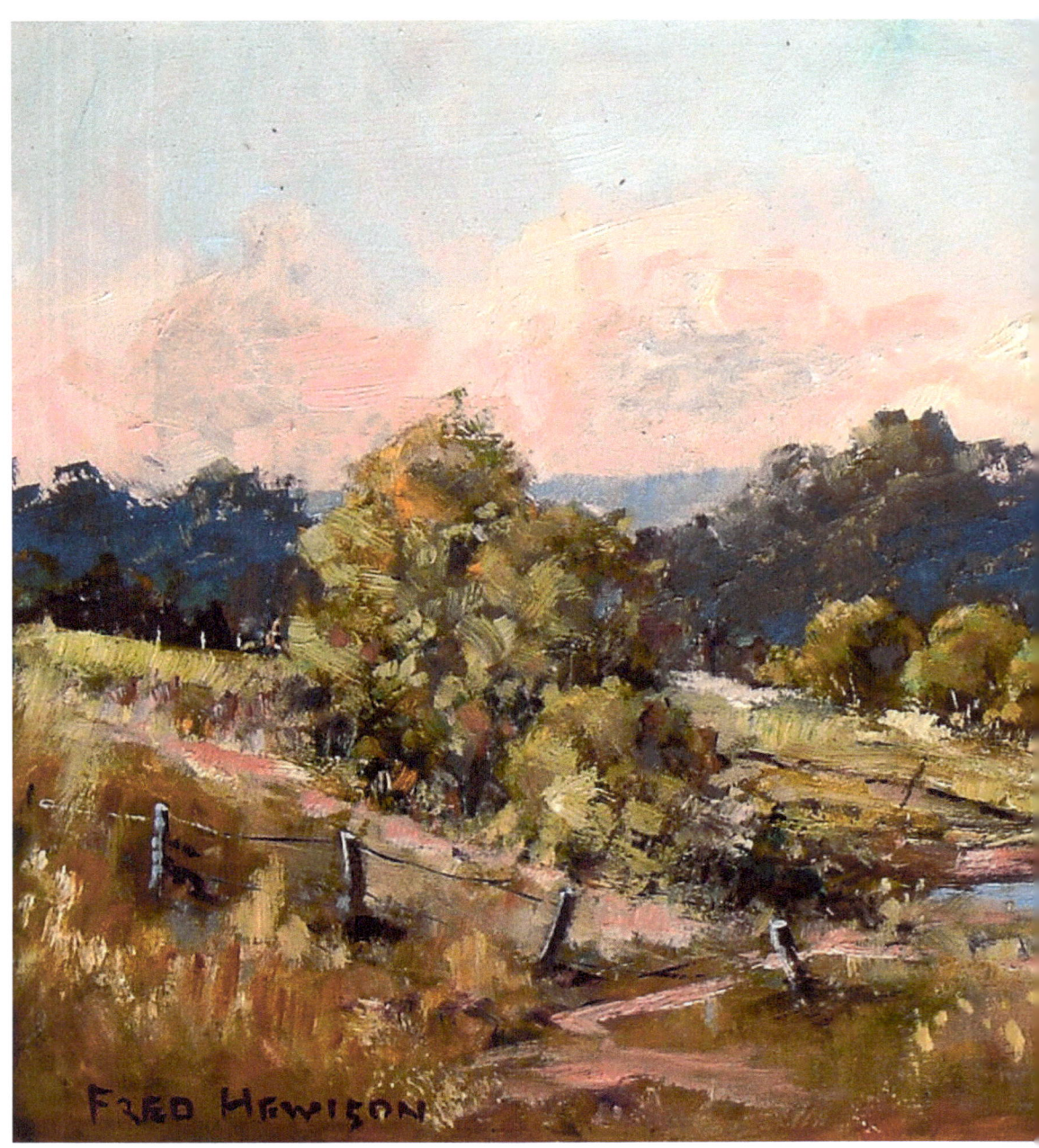

Copmanhurst, NSW

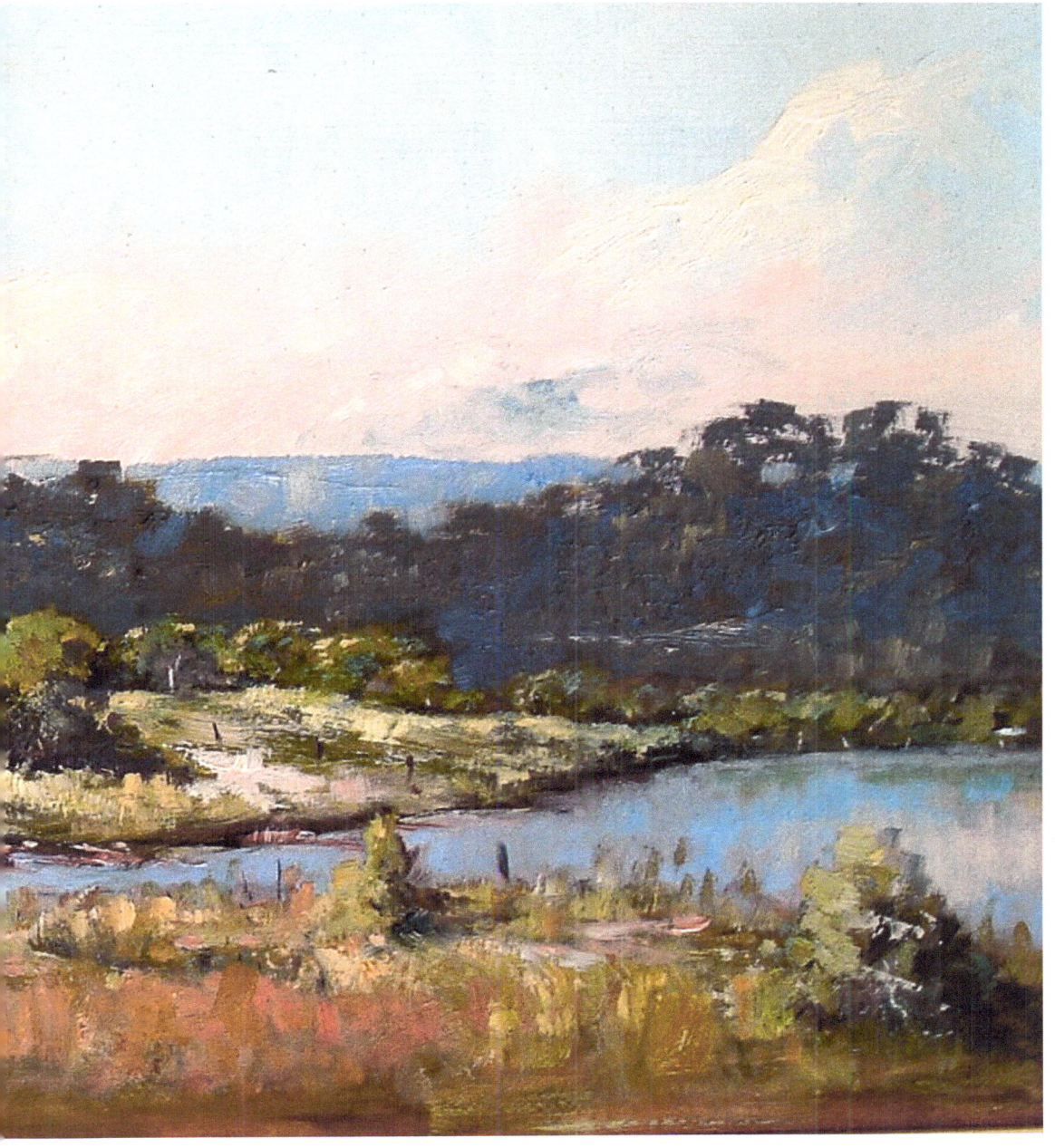

www.ingramcontent.com/pod-product-compliance
Lightning Source LLC
Chambersburg PA
CBHW041939240526
45473CB00037B/2394